Classic Gatwick
JETLINERS

CLASSIC GATWICK JETLINERS

TOM SINGFIELD

The History Press

Frontispiece: A line up of heavies in August 1984 that will never be repeated at Gatwick. Five Boeing 747s from different airlines – Cathay Pacific, Philippine Airlines, British Caledonian, Air New Zealand and Air Lanka. (Mike Axe)

First published 2021
Reprinted 2024

The History Press
97 St George's Place, Cheltenham,
Gloucestershire, GL50 3QB
www.thehistorypress.co.uk

British Library Cataloguing in Publication Data.
A catalogue record for this book is available from the British Library.

ISBN 978 0 7509 9424 8

Typesetting and origination by The History Press
Printed by TJ Books Limited, Padstow, Cornwall

MIX
Paper from
responsible sources
FSC
www.fsc.org   FSC® C013056

CONTENTS

ACKNOWLEDGEMENTS & THANKS

First I must thank my long time friend Bernard King for kindly agreeing to write the foreword. Bernard was for many years the Chairman of the Gatwick Aviation Society and a great supporter of Gatwick airport with a close knowledge of its staff, its workings and many of its historic events. Bernard sadly passed away in December 2022 leaving a huge gap in the number of people who had intimate knowledge of historic Gatwick operations.

Many of the friends who supplied images or loaned slides for *Classic Gatwick Propliners* have once again come up with the goods. Without their skills and generosity, this book would have been impossible to complete and certainly not as colourful and wide ranging. I would like to especially thank Jacques Guillem in Paris who provided some wonderful images from his incredible slide collection prior to his untimely death in April 2023. Thanks too to Tim Spearman for an impressive piece of slide enhancement.

Thanks to the following for their help with images. Ian Anderson, Mike Axe, Adrian Balch, Peter Bish, Brooklands Museum, Keith Brooks, Keith Butcher, Caz Caswell, Barry Collman, John Crawford, Ron Cuskelly, Geoff Dobson, Tony Eastwood – AJ Aviation, Martin Fenner, Ken Fielding, Steve Fowler, Dave Freeman, Clive Grant, Barry Guess BAe Systems, Peter Guiver, David Hedges, Scott Henderson, Roy Hobbs, Guy Holman, Richard Hunt, Tony Hyatt, Tony Merton Jones, Bernard King, Chris Knott – Air Photographic International, Andy Marsh, Peter Marson, John Mounce, John Murray, Bob O'Brien, Steve Ozel, Terry Rattue, Glen Reid, Robin Ridley, Paul Robinson, Paul Sheehan, Tim Spearman, Ian Terry, David Thaxter, Richard Vandervord, Christian Volpati, Bob Wall, Jonathan Walton, Pete Waterfield, Steve Williams and Stephen Wolf.

A special thanks to my old Gatwick Aviation Society colleagues who have provided much of the background information used in compiling the photo captions and even proof reading them to weed out the spelling errors and "duff gen". Harry Hawkins, Ken Ede, John Dyer, Paul Hayes at Cirium and Keith Palmer. Their impressive knowledge of early Gatwick aircraft movements, routes and fleets have been invaluable. Thanks too to Ewan Partridge and Peter Hillman for help with captions.

Finally I should like to thank my wife Maggi for tolerating my passion for aviation for over 50 years. Without her support in the background I would certainly not have become an aviation writer and had the freedom to travel, research and write in my little office for so many years.

Tom Singfield
Horsham
February 2024

FOREWORD

I was delighted to be asked by Tom to write the foreword to this book. His previous work *Classic Gatwick Propliners*, published in 2019, brought back so many wonderful memories of those happy and innocent days of aircraft spotting at Gatwick long before security fences and airport expansion spoilt everything.

The revitalised Gatwick Airport was officially opened by the Queen on Monday, 9 June 1958 and, less than four months later, BOAC inaugurated transatlantic jet services with De Havilland Comet 4s between Heathrow and New York on Saturday, 4 October 1958. G-APDB operated the eastbound service while G-APDC flew London to New York on the same morning. Gatwick-based Dan-Air London played a significant role in the type's later history and at one time owned all forty-nine remaining airworthy civilian Comets, including both G-APDB and G-APDC, which joined their fleet in autumn 1969 after a four-year stint with Malaysian Airlines.

By the end of November 1958, Gatwick had seen its first visit by a jetliner in the form of a BOAC Comet 4 on diversion from a fog-enshrouded Heathrow. As the secondary London airport, Gatwick rarely received regular visits by jetliners. For example, the movements for August 1963 reveal that there were only five jetliner visits to Gatwick that month, an RAF Comet plus a short series of charter flights from and to Helsinki using Finnair Caravelles.

British United Airways was formed in July 1960 and its large fleet of ninety-two propeller aircraft was nominally based at Gatwick under the management of aviation entrepreneur Freddie Laker. His announcement of an order for ten BAC 1-11 short-range airliners straight off the drawing board the following May was a surprise for everybody. BUA also ordered two VC10 convertible cargo-passenger aircraft for operation on its African and South American scheduled services. The first of these, G-ASIW, was officially handed over to the airline on 30 September 1964, although a combined route-proving, publicity and crew-training flight was made to various capital cities in Central Africa departing Gatwick on 14 September. The previous day, the VC10 had made a one-day appearance at the Farnborough Air Show and opened its large forward freight door to reveal a Rolls-Royce Silver Cloud III motor car loaned by the manufacturer and appropriately registered RR1. This prompted Laker, forever the publicist, to inform the press that the African continent would be the first to witness a 600mph motor car!

The first BAC 1-11 to arrive at Gatwick was actually the ninth of BUA's order and G-ASJI commenced an intensive series of route-proving flights on 25 January 1965, visiting mainly Genoa, Jersey, Malaga and Palma. Usually aboard these flights were the cockpit crew, a number of Civil Aviation Authority observers and two cabin crew members to provide safety briefings and serve refreshments. Aboard the late-night flight to Malaga on 13 February 1965 were two interlopers (myself included) who gained the dubious honour of being the first ever passengers on a BAC 1-11, and on return, received the writer's only ever ride in a police car!

Also in 1965, the airport saw the first regular passenger operations by overseas companies in the form of Capitol DC-8s and Continental Airlines Boeing 707s. These operated what were known as affinity group charters, which were a way of getting around the strictly enforced and highly inflated fares charged by members of the International Air Transport Association to which most government-owned airlines belonged. This led to charters being organised by some interesting but bizarrely named groups such as the 'Tortoise Athletics Association'!

The first scheduled jet flights by an overseas carrier were those operated by Kingdom of Libya Airlines from Tripoli, using Caravelles and starting on 1 April 1966. On Saturday, 13 April 1969, a group of aircraft spotters and I descended on Gatwick to await the arrival of Aérolíneas Peruanas (APSA) Douglas DC-8-52 OB-R-931, which would be the first Peruvian-registered aeroplane to hit the log book. We were all upset to learn that the flight was delayed until the following day 'due to technical issues in Madrid'. Not only were we disappointed but so also were the world's press, who had been invited to report on the carrier's first transatlantic operation. One enterprising reporter from Radio Luxembourg decided to interview me to fill the scheduled slot and my cousin Zena, honeymooning away from it all in a caravan in Pembrokeshire, got the surprise of her life when hearing about plane spotting at Gatwick on the radio!

I first met Tom more than fifty years ago, probably on a patch of grass we called 'The Green', not far from the General Aviation Terminal (GAT) where we spotters played cricket and football for many years until the BAA removed our squatters' rights in order to build what we now know as the North Terminal. Tom spent much of his working life as an air traffic controller at Gatwick Airport, which allowed him airside access to take many of the images illustrating this book from the better side of the fence! He has spent many years sourcing other superb images, and the interesting captions, much aided by information published in the Gatwick Aviation Society's monthly publication *Hawkeye*, help make this a superb companion to his earlier volume.

Bernie King
Founder & Chairman
Gatwick Aviation Society 1967–2017

INTRODUCTION

Welcome to *Classic Gatwick Jetliners*, a companion volume for the successful *Classic Gatwick Propliners* first published by The History Press in April 2019. This volume switches its focus to the amazing selection of classic civil jetliners that have appeared at Gatwick since it opened on the present site in 1958. This book covers the first thirty years of Gatwick up to 1988, so most of the types illustrated are no longer in service and many of the airlines and operators are now just distant memories.

Having made its first flight at Hatfield on 23 September 1958, BOAC's Comet 4 G-APDC made Gatwick history when it became the first jetliner to ever land there. On its way from Dublin to Heathrow on 16 November that year, it was one of six aircraft (the others were four Viscounts and a Britannia) that diverted into Gatwick due to foggy conditions at Heathrow. It landed at 1226 and once the fog had lifted, it took off for Heathrow at 1444. In 1965, BOAC sold G-APDC in Malaysia as 9M-AOC and in August 1969 it returned to be based at Gatwick after it was bought by Dan-Air London. Its last service for Dan-Air was on 10 April 1973. Diversions of all types to Gatwick from Heathrow and other airports in those early days were not uncommon, with seventy-six in the last six months of 1958, 266 in 1959 and 141 in 1960.

▲ Gatwick's first recorded jetliner visit was BOAC's de Havilland Comet 4 G-APDC, which diverted in from Heathrow in November 1958. (Author's collection)

The first scheduled jetliner service to use Gatwick is usually quoted as British United Airways' long-haul VC10 schedule to Santiago, which initially flew as a route-proving/sales tour in October 1964 followed by the official first schedule on 5 November. However, it may be that Swissair should really take the credit as it started a weekly summertime Sunday night Caravelle service from Zurich in June 1964.

Other early regular jetliners that first appeared in the mid 1960s included the BUA BAC 1-11 fleet, Aeroflot Tupolev Tu-104s, Britannia Boeing 737s, lots of Caravelles including those from Sterling, Scandinavian Airlines System (SAS), Kingdom of Libya Airlines and Iberia, Trans International DC-8s, Continental Boeing 707s, World Boeing 707s, the Wardair Boeing 727 and not forgetting an airline and type that was synonymous with Gatwick for many years – Dan-Air London with its magnificent fleet of de Havilland Comets.

As larger and longer-range jetliners used Gatwick, it became obvious to the airport operator that the runway would need to be lengthened from its original 7,000ft, so in 1964 work commenced to lengthen it to 8,200ft. The British Airports Authority took over the running of Gatwick in 1966 and was told by some long-haul airlines that they were not able to use Gatwick with full loads so a further extension to 9,075ft was made in 1970, followed by yet another extension to 10,165ft in 1973 that needed a public enquiry to get the go-ahead. Various plans for a second runway go back to the 1960s but, apart from the conversion of the main parallel taxiway into an 'emergency' runway available in the event of the main runway being out of action for a long time, a second runway has yet to appear, and with the 2020 collapse of traffic thanks to Covid-19, it is likely that a two-runway Gatwick design as shown in artists' renditions will be quietly filed away for later.

A consequence of the appearance of wide-body jetliners at Gatwick (and elsewhere) from the early

▲ Interesting view from the ATC Ground Movement Control office in the South Terminal in July 1981. Note the varied selection of wide-bodied jetliner types parked up on the centre pier with smaller airliners including a CTA Caravelle, Scimitar Boeing 707, the Dan-Air Training Comet and lots of 1-11s and 737s filling many of the parking spaces. (Author)

1970s was the introduction of 'vortex wake' separation behind large jets on approach to the airport. From 1974, all aircraft were put into categories depending on their maximum take-off weight; these were named Heavy, Medium, Small and Light. The paper Flight Progress Strips used in Air Traffic Control (ATC) started to show the aircraft type followed by a letter indicating its vortex wake category – H, M, S and L. For example, H – Boeing 747, M – Boeing 707, S – Viscount, L – Piper Navajo. If there was no outbound aircraft to get away in the 'gap' between two arrivals, then the Approach Radar Controller could position an inbound aircraft at a certain distance behind the preceding aircraft according to a table that went from 'No vortex wake separation required', when any category of aircraft followed a 'Light', to no less than 8 miles when a 'Light' followed a 'Heavy'. With Gatwick's famous mix of traffic, which back then included everything from single-seat light aircraft to a Boeing 747, you can see that sometimes the spacing between inbounds could cause arrival delays. These could be reduced by 'juggling' the inbound sequence to avoid the worst spacing requirements. Over the years the categories have been amended with the likes of Concorde and now the Airbus A380 causing a huge vortex wake behind them. A modified vortex wake separation table is still in force but not at Heathrow Approach Radar, where in 2015 they introduced time-based separation technology that takes into account the ground speed of the inbound aircraft as well as their vortex category to help Air Traffic Control Officers (ATCOs) correctly space inbound aircraft. All highly technical but it works well; look it up, it's called eTBS – Enhanced Time-Based Separation.

It's probably true that many aircraft enthusiasts back in the 1960s and '70s preferred Gatwick to Heathrow because of its eclectic mix of traffic. It was never as busy as Heathrow, but the visitors walking out on to the viewing deck were never sure what they would see at Gatwick, unlike Heathrow, where most movements were scheduled. In those days, Gatwick was also popular with owners of light aircraft and the occasional business jet, who all made use of the extensive parking by the single-storey General Aviation Terminal (opened in 1966) while out flying on a 'jolly' or quite often to clear Customs when routing to or

▲ A summer outing to Gatwick to watch the planes was a popular pastime for many families in the 1960s and '70s. This view from the South Pier deck in July 1971 shows just how close to the action visitors could get, all for the price of a cup of tea. This is World Airways Douglas DC-8 Series 63 N802WA, which was destroyed in a crash in Alaska two years later. (Author's collection)

from airfields outside of the UK. An interesting statistic is that in 1966, one fifth of all the movements at Gatwick were business and light aircraft. Photos show that in the summer of 1969, light aircraft movements overwhelmed the spaces available at the GAT so some were parked on a grass area opposite the North Park.

Thanks to Gatwick's popular spectators' viewing deck, the accessibility for enthusiasts, photographers and the general public in the 1960s and '70s was superb. Providing the aircraft were parked conveniently, friends and families could use the open decks to wave off passengers as they walked out to their aircraft, as there were no air bridges until the centre finger was extensively updated in 1977.

I started my Air Traffic Controller career at Gatwick in 1978 and once I had obtained an airside driving permit I was able to borrow the Civil Aviation Authority (CAA) van during my breaks to go and shoot some slides of whatever was on the airport. I was fortunate to be allowed to 'free range' on the airport and go anywhere airside other than the runway. This freedom allowed me to position myself for the best shots. I have to own up that sometimes a fellow enthusiast on Ground Movement Control would give an inbound/outbound aircraft a taxiway route that ensured it was positioned in the perfect place for a photo. The favourite time to shoot an aircraft was after push back with the tug gone and the aircraft awaiting taxi clearance. That ensured a clear shot and enough time to shoot some extra slides to exchange with friends around the world. If a particularly interesting airliner was pushed back in full sunlight then you could sometimes be surrounded by several like-minded Gatwick workers all snapping away merrily!

Looking back over the years that I have been involved with Gatwick both as an enthusiast and as an Air Traffic Controller, the 1980s were amazing times for the airport with huge growth in passenger numbers and aircraft movements. Much of this growth was due to a change of government in 1979, as this amended the policy of directing operators to switch to Gatwick and instead encouraged them to move there by reducing landing and other fees. In addition, the government stated that no new international airline would be allowed to operate from Heathrow. The consequential influx of airlines saw passenger numbers increase considerably. In 1979 total passengers were around 8.5 million; this had jumped to nearly 21 million by 1988, the cut-off date for this book.

I should make a short apology for not including a few biz jets in this volume but sadly there wasn't enough room. Gatwick's first business jet was arguably a French Air Force MS760 Paris back in April 1959 but if you wanted to see a 'true' biz jet then you had to wait for the first visit of a Lockheed JetStar in March 1962, when a US-registered example passed through on delivery to the Indonesian Air Force.

▲ The clatter of non-digital cameras drowns out the sound of an aircraft starting up adjacent to the South Pier. The passengers on the aircraft must have wondered just what was so special about their aircraft to warrant such attention from a gang of aviation photographers who probably should have been at work! (Author)

I was also unable to include many of the surprising number of military jetliners that visited during the period covered by this book. Probably the most common were the regular appearances of the five Canadian military Boeing 707s that they referred to as CC-137s. The Royal Canadian Air Force's first jetliner was the DH Comet and both of its Comet 1Xs made several visits from 1959 until 1963. Other military Boeing 707 types came from Iran, Israel, the USA and Germany. The Americans also appeared with C-141 Starlifters, KC-10s (DC-10s) and C-9s (DC-9s). The RAF visited with Comets, TriStars, HS146s, BAC 1-11s and VC10s. The biggest military jetliner to visit was a Boeing 747-100 of the Imperial Iranian Air Force in September 1975.

▼ An example of the military jetliners that visited is Boeing CC-137 13701 of the Canadian Armed Forces in September 1970. Newly delivered to Canada in 1970, it flew with them for twenty-four years. (Author's collection)

▲ Seen from the BAA Apron Control Office on the ninth floor of the terminal building, DC-10 demonstrator N1338U negotiates the right turn from Taxiway 2 to Taxiway 1. Note all the logos of the airlines that had ordered the DC-10 from McDonnell Douglas. (Keith Brooks)

▲ With the advent of the low-cost carriers swamping the parking stands at Gatwick, will we ever see such a colourful variety of jetliners again? All the airlines in this August 1988 view have ceased to exist apart from Air Zimbabwe, which was just hanging on in 2020. (Author)

The first wide-body type to drop in at Gatwick was the brand-new McDonnell Douglas DC-10 demonstrator N1338U on 10 August 1972, having visited Heathrow the day before for BEA to look at it. This was followed just seven days later by its competitor, Lockheed's L-1011 TriStar demonstrator N305EA. The first Boeing 747 to visit was South African Airways' ZS-SAM on 1 November 1972.

This book was completed in the midst of the Covid-19 pandemic. At that time, air transport movements at Gatwick were virtually at a standstill, and the repercussions in the world of aviation will be with us for years to come. While the skies are quiet, airlines will fail, workers will lose their jobs and my favourite airport will struggle to get back to its former busy days. Gatwick was famous for being the world's busiest single runway airport, and before the virus hit, my ex-colleagues in ATC were 'shifting' more than 950 movements in a twenty-four-hour period during the summer months. It is unlikely that those figures will be beaten now, at least not for several years. I hope the images and stories in this book will recall the 'good old' days for many of you who visited Gatwick, especially those like me who have a special attachment to this remarkable airport in the Sussex countryside.

Tom Singfield
Horsham
June 2020

1

THE SIXTIES

The appearance of a jetliner at Gatwick in the early 1960s was a rare sight; these were usually diversions from other airports. At that time, British United Airways was the big player with 800,000 of Gatwick's 1,000,000 passengers using BUA propliners in 1962. Gatwick's status as a 'bucket and spade' airport was enhanced when the Ministry for Aviation transferred all regular charter flights from Heathrow to Gatwick in 1963. By the mid 1960s, BUA had started to receive its brand new BAC 1-11s and its VC10s were delighting passengers on long-haul flights to the other side of the world. US transatlantic charter airlines started to switch to DC-8 and Boeing 707 jetliners and with the setting up of the independent British Airports Authority to control the London airports in 1966,

the future for Gatwick was very bright. Some readers may remember arriving at the terminal by driving up a one-way ramp to a small roundabout that was positioned above the main A23 road. I can remember parking right outside and popping in to see what aircraft were due to arrive. The access to a direct rail line to London was, and still is, a huge boost for passenger numbers. However they arrived, the check-in desks were just inside the terminal and it was just a short walk to the two-storey single pier where their aircraft waited. The jet age slowly arrived at Gatwick and with it many sleepless nights for the locals, especially on summer weekends, when the continuous night-time services were operated by some horribly noisy first-generation jets.

◄ Part of its initial order for ten BAC One-Elevens in 1961, BUA's Series 201AC G-ASJI made a pre-delivery visit to Gatwick on 13 February 1965 when it flew to Malaga and back with some CAA personnel and a couple of hangers on! It was officially delivered to BUA on 15 April 1965. Six days earlier, sister ship G-ASJJ flew the world's first commercial service by a BAC 1-11 when it flew Gatwick to Genoa. By 1967 the BUA fleet was all turbine, serving thirty-two destinations in nineteen countries, but by 1969 profits were falling and, with no help from a sickly Labour government, BUA's owners tried to sell out to BOAC. A new Conservative government allowed new negotiations and in the end BUA was sold to Caledonian in October 1970 for £6.9 million. The name Caledonian//BUA hung around until September 1972, when it became British Caledonian. G-ASJI was sold to Pacific Express in the USA and succumbed to the scrap man around 2015 in Lubumbashi, DRC, after flying for Air Katanga. It had amassed over 47,000 hours' flying time. (Christian Volpati collection)

▲ The Kingdom of Libya Airlines (KoLA) was an international airline established in 1964 serving the Mediterranean and major destinations in Europe and the Middle East with scheduled flights from Libya. The airline made its first revenue flight in October 1965 using a Caravelle, and although many foreign airlines were reticent to use Gatwick, KoLA inaugurated Caravelle services to Tripoli from 1 April 1966. By 1968, the international network included destinations such as Athens, Beirut, Cairo, Geneva, London, Paris, Rome and Tunis, which were served using either Caravelle or Fokker F27 aircraft. The airline also had inter-line agreements with Alitalia, MEA and BOAC. In 1969, the airline was renamed Libyan Arab Airlines and in the summer of 1970 the schedules were switched to Heathrow. One of three Caravelles VI-Rs in the fleet, 5A-DAA was first seen at Gatwick in June 1966 on the weekly Saturday service from Tripoli via Geneva. Note the not-so-sleek Dan-Air Bristol Freighter G-AINL on the South Park behind. (Author's collection)

➤ Palma-based TAE (Trabajos Aéreos y Enlaces S.A.) was set up to fly IT packages and started ops in April 1967 using a Douglas DC-7C. In order to better compete with other jet-equipped fleets, the airline ordered two BAC 1-11 Series 402APs from a cancelled Philippine Airlines order. The first, EC-BQF 'Nervion', was delivered in March 1969 but the second, although painted in TAE's colours, was never delivered. EC-BQF, seen here still with its Philippine registration PI-C1151, became the first jetliner to be operated by TAE and the only 1-11 to be registered in Spain. It managed less than a year flying package holidays in Europe until it was repossessed by the manufacturer in February 1970. TAE suspended operations shortly afterwards but a new TAE iteration would return to Gatwick in 1973 when it was refinanced and re-formed with three DC-8s. However, operating fuel-thirsty jetliners was not good for company finances and the airline filed for bankruptcy in 1982. (Stephen Wolf collection)

◄ This very simple colour scheme was applied to the first Boeing 737s bought by Luton-based Britannia Airways in 1968. In fact, Britannia was the first European charter airline to buy new Boeing 737-200s with G-AVRL (the first of its type registered in the UK) making its first Gatwick appearance on 29 July 1968. Britannia Airways had commenced IT charters to European holiday destinations from Gatwick in March that year, using Bristol Britannias on behalf of the parent travel company, Thomsons. Note the catering containers being loaded/offloaded by a Dan-Air Commer Karrier, a rare truck these days. G-AVRL ended her days in the USA, finally being scrapped in 1993. (Author's collection)

▲ Aérolíneas Peruanas (APSA) was founded by C.W. Shelton in September 1956 with flights using Curtiss C-46 Commandos from Lima to Miami and Santiago commencing in mid 1957. By 1963 the airline was flying Convair 990As but it wasn't until APSA acquired Douglas DC-8s in 1969 that it could commence transatlantic services. DC-8-52 OB-R-931 first arrived at LGW (twelve hours late due technical problems in Madrid) as flight number EP222 on 13 April 1969. The late arrival was a bit embarrassing for APSA as the world's press were waiting for it. Schedules were due in on Tuesday and out on Wednesday and in Saturday/ out Sunday. The airline managed to get approval to switch services to Heathrow in July 1970 but stopped all flying on 2 May 1971, leaving the Peruvian military government without a national carrier. This led to the creation of AeroPerú, which then attempted to compete against the big US airlines for traffic to and from Lima. (Author's collection)

◄ American Flyers Airline (AFA) was formed at Fort Worth in Texas way back in 1939 as a pilot training school. It flew DC-3/C-47s on charters from 1949 and was granted US Supplemental Carrier status in 1959. It commenced services using Lockheed Constellations in 1960 followed by Lockheed L188 Electras in 1963, both types visiting Gatwick. Early in 1968 it took delivery of a pair of new Boeing 727-185Cs (N12826 and N12827) for passenger charters and both appeared at Gatwick regularly on summer transatlantic charters over the next two years. AFA was the very first airline to operate 727s on transatlantic services. N12826 is seen parked on the centre pier on 30 August 1969 after arriving from Gander; it later departed to Keflavik. The airline part of AFA was taken over by Universal Airlines in May 1971 but the pilot training continues to this day. (Steve Williams)

► Caravelle III PH-TRM of Dutch charter specialist Transavia Holland is seen here in 1969, soon after joining the airline in its first year of operating jets. Transavia expanded rapidly from its 1966 beginnings with a couple of Douglas DC-6s and in the summer season of 1967 it flew 21,000 passengers, followed by more than 60,000 the following year. It operated a total of fourteen different Caravelles that became a common sight at many European airports associated with charter activity. PH-TRM was leased from Sud Aviation for only fifteen months and was eventually scrapped in the Congo in 1996. To the rear can be seen one of Caledonian Airways' original pair of Boeing 707-399Cs, often overlooked as being the first 707s based at Gatwick. (Jacques Guillem collection)

◄ Parked up at the end of the North Pier on 31 July 1969 is Trans International Airways' (TIA) Boeing 727-171C N1727T, one of the few 727s that were flown to Gatwick on transatlantic charters in the late 1960s and early '70s along with American Flyers, Wardair and World Airways. N1727T and TIA's other 727 N1728T were Quick Change passenger/freight 'Combi' versions with main deck cargo doors and were delivered new to TIA in April and June 1968. Both aircraft first appeared at LGW in June 1969 and continued to drop in for the rest of the year. After a lease to Braniff in 1972–74, N1727T was sold to Pacific Western in Canada. TIA, based in Oakland, California, flew transatlantic charters between 1966 and 1986, later using Boeing 747s, DC-8s and DC-10s. (Ken Fielding)

▲ Some brave Gatwick enthusiasts would stay on the viewing decks after they were officially closed so they could catch a rare arrival in the dark. Even braver were those who tried a time exposure without a tripod to catch one of these movements on film. This 1967-built BAC 1-11 420EL arrived at Gatwick from Wisley carrying the delivery registration LV-PID en route to Austral in Argentina on 12 October 1967. It departed via Keflavik the next day and on arrival was re-registered LV-IZR. The aircraft had already appeared at LGW as G-AVTF while returning from Romania after demonstrations to TAROM in August that year. Amazingly it reappeared at Gatwick in February 1986 in Quebecair colours prior to moving on to Okada Air the same month. (Bernard King)

➤ Following the shutdown of the much-loved British Eagle in November 1968, its two Boeing 707-138Bs G-AVZZ 'Enterprise' and G-AWDG 'Phoenix' went into storage until they were sold by the liquidators to Freddie Laker so he could replace his two Britannias. G-AWDG was delivered to Gatwick in February 1969 but didn't enter airline service until May due to crew training requirements. Laker used them on transatlantic services, although from 1970 G-AVZZ was leased to International Caribbean Airlines, which was a joint Laker/Barbados government venture and was painted with their titles. G-AWDG covered for it when it was under overhaul. (David Hedges collection)

▲ Every new VC10, this is G-ASIW, made its first flight from the Vickers factory at Weybridge/Brooklands to the facility at Wisley where final fitting out was done. With just a light fuel load, the take-off from the short 1,460-yard runway was always impressive and, unless some flight testing was carried out, the aircraft could be on the ground at Wisley in five minutes. Costing British United Airways £2.8 million each, the long-haul Vickers VC10 entered service on 1 October 1964 on an MoD trooping flight to Nairobi. The following month, BUA became the first private UK carrier to begin scheduled jet operations from Gatwick when it commenced services to Rio, Montevideo, Buenos Aires and Santiago with a twice-weekly VC10 with alternate stops in Madrid and Lisbon. The VC10s carried ninety-three tourist-class and nineteen first-class passengers along with 5 tons of freight on the twelve-hour journey. (BAe Systems)

◄ Perhaps not a 'perfect' shot, but this is an iconic view taken from the North Pier of Stand 36 along with a nice selection of light aircraft parked on the grass as well as three Britannias and a Dakota in the distance. The first 707 for Caledonian was this 707-399C G-AVKA. Reported as originally carrying the name 'County of Ayr', it first flew in July 1967 before being immediately leased to Flying Tiger Line for a year as N319F still in partial Caledonian colours. By the time of this photo in October 1969 it had been renamed 'Flagship Bonnie Scotland'. From late 1970 it was given Caledonian/BUA titles, followed a year later by British Caledonian titles. Sold to TAP Air Portugal in 1973, it later went through a long list of freight airlines until it was scrapped at Luanda around 2010. (Author's collection)

► In the summer of 1965, Gatwick saw the arrival of a summer season of mostly weekend transatlantic charters by Continental Airlines using its fabulous Boeing 707 'Intercontinental Golden Jets'. Most appear to have departed originally from Los Angeles and returned with a fuel stop in Montreal or Shannon. Some flights continued eastbound into Europe with Orly, Le Bourget, Amsterdam, Frankfurt and Rome noted. Four-month-old 707-324C N17324 is seen here on 14 September 1965, just as the season was ending. Altogether eight different Continental 707s visited during three summers of services. During 1966 and 1967, Toronto was often used for the fuel stop eastbound. N17324 was sold to China Airlines and was destroyed in September 1979 when it flew into the sea while crew training. (Chris Knott collection)

▲ A stunning view of Dan-Air London Comet 4 G-APDO taken one afternoon in the summer of 1967 off the 1,000ft-long North Pier, which was completed in 1963. Note the construction work on the office block above the terminal (now South Terminal) building. Dan-Air initially bought two BOAC de Havilland Comet 4s (G-APDK and this one, G-APDO) in 1966. These were modified at Lasham to carry ninety-nine passengers for IT operations by Clarkson and Horizon. G-APDO flew Dan-Air's first Comet service from Gatwick to Barcelona on 16 November 1966. Remarkably, Dan-Air was still flying Comets fourteen years later and the last ever commercial Comet service in the world was an Ian Allan enthusiasts' flight from Gatwick to Gatwick with G-BDIW on 9 November 1980. A company employee later calculated that Dan-Air's Comets had flown 238,000 hours, the equivalent of 95,400,000 miles! By 1980, Dan-Air had owned or operated forty-nine of the seventy-six Comet 4/4B/4C aircraft built. (Author's collection)

▲ This 1967 model Boeing 707-355C was leased by International Air Bahama from Executive Jet Aviation in July 1968 and made its first appearance at Gatwick on 8 July 1969. Formed in 1966 by British financier and property developer Norman Ricketts, it originally ordered two DC-8-63s for a low-cost scheduled service to Luxembourg. However, this aircraft order lapsed and the airline reportedly made its first flight from Nassau to Luxembourg on 20 July 1968, so the visit on 8 July may have been a route-proving flight. The airline subsequently flew thrice weekly, stopping in Bermuda eastbound and Shannon, Gander or Santa Maria westbound using the leased 707. The airline was taken over in August 1969 by a subsidiary of Loftleidir and the route was subsequently flown by their own DC-8s. This aircraft reappeared at Gatwick in 1970, when it was leased by Caledonian Airways as G-AYEX. It returned to EJA in September 1971 and ended its flying days as an EC-137D with the US Air Force. (Author's collection)

➤ On every Sunday morning during the summer (June to September) of 1965, a Sudan Airways de Havilland Comet positioned over from Heathrow at around 0900Z before operating a service to Tangier and back on behalf of British United using flight numbers BR249/BR250. It then returned to Heathrow the same evening. Here is ST-AAW taxying outbound on Sunday, 18 July 1965 for its service to Tangier. It had been delivered to Sudan Airways in November 1962 and the airline became the last ever civil Comet operator to serve Heathrow in November 1972. Both Sudan Comet 4Cs (the other was ST-AAX) were bought by Dan-Air London in June 1975 and flown back to the UK. ST-AAW became G-ASDZ and was broken up for spares at Lasham, while ST-AAX flew with Dan-Air for a few years as G-BDIF. (Peter Marson)

◄ Vancouver-based Pacific Western Airlines (PWA) was an early operator with jetliners to Gatwick with its 1959-built Boeing 707-138B CF-PWV (seen here) first arriving at LGW in May 1968. This year saw PWA compete with Canadian Pacific DC-8-40s (DC-8-60s from 1969) and Wardair with its new 707-300s. This short-bodied 707-138 was unable to make the westbound Atlantic crossing without a fuel stop at either Keflavik or more often Søndre Strømfjord in Greenland, hardly a good advert for PWA's service. It leased another short-bodied138B from 1969 to 1971, then bought a Series 321C in July 1972 but this crashed the following January and was replaced by 707-351C CF-PWJ two months later. CF-PWV was sold in October 1978 to Tiger Air and ended up as a VIP machine for Prince Bandar of Saudi Arabia as HZ-123. (Ron Cuskelly collection)

▲ Now here is a Canadian airline with connections to Gatwick going right back to the 1960s when Nordair appeared with a DC-4, a DC-7 and its wonderful Super Constellations. Jet charters from Canada started in 1968 when Nordair leased this immaculate Convair 990 Coronado N5615 from Modern Air Transport. Interestingly Nordair could only manage transatlantic CV990 flights after deciding that speed was less important than range. Flown at Mach 0.78 instead of 0.85, they saved 38 per cent of fuel burn and increased the range by 20 per cent! Nordair flew DC-8s to Gatwick from 1975 after the Coronados (it leased two others from MAT) had been withdrawn. Nordair was put up for sale in 1977 but political interference and other problems dragged out the deal for ten years until CP Air took it over in 1987. (Jacques Guillem collection)

◄ Shot from the North Pier on 28 August 1966, Air Algérie's Caravelle VI-N 7T-VAK was on a sub-charter for Aviaco of Spain. These Sunday summertime charters to/from Palma only appeared in 1966. 7T-VAK had flown with the company from new as F-OBNK prior to adopting the 7T prefix in 1964. Sadly it came to a tragic end when en route from Marseilles to Hassi-Messaoud in Algeria via Algiers on a charter flight 26 July 1969. An electrical short circuit in the cockpit caused so much smoke that the crew declared an emergency and diverted towards Biskra airport, but the crew lost control and it crashed in flames 40km from the airport. Thirty-three of the thirty-seven occupants were killed. Air Algérie had flown Caravelles from 1960, with the last one being retired in 1976. (Barry Collman)

▲ According to available documents, the earliest Swissair Caravelle flights to Gatwick can be dated to December 1962 when both HB-ICU and HB-ICV appeared on charters. Then in 1964, prior to commencing a once-weekly Caravelle service from Zurich Kloten on 7 June, Swissair flew a couple of 'proving flights' from Zurich that April with HB-ICR and HB-ICX. The regular Sunday night Caravelle flights arrived at 0100 as SR1930 and were off again as SR1931 after a one-hour turn round. This 'schedule' finished on 20 September but returned the following summer. In 1966, the frequencies increased and Geneva was added but they still arrived in the middle of the night and, depending on loads, sometimes the Caravelles were swapped for Coronados, DC-8s or DC-9s. This set-up continued in 1967 and 1968 but with DC-9s appearing more often. I put the word 'schedule' in inverted commas as there is some debate about these flights being scheduled or just regular charters. (Jacques Guillem collection)

➤ Starting out in 1953 with a single Douglas DC-3 Dakota, then adding a pair of Curtiss 'Super' C-46s, Transair Sweden started holiday charter flights for the summer season in 1957. Based at Malmö, Transair Sweden grew its fleet of the venerable C-46 to ten aircraft. These were joined by Douglas DC-6Bs and later DC-7Bs, which were better suited to IT flights to the Mediterranean hot spots. The airline's first jets were three Boeing 727-100 'Sunjets' but their range wasn't marvellous and they had to refuel en route to the Canary Islands. In 1968, when this shot of SE-DDB 'Northern Light' was taken, the 727s were flown on behalf of Scanair. SAS bought out Transair in 1975 but it continued to fly under its own name until it went into liquidation in late 1981. This aircraft flew into a mountain in Ecuador in 2002 while flying with TAME. (Author's collection)

◄ Such a simple yet elegant colour scheme on this 'Flying pencil' Douglas DC-8-61CF N8956U of Saturn Airways at Gatwick in 1968. Delivered brand new in January that year, N8956U was a regular transatlantic charter machine alongside other DC-8 operators from the USA including Capitol, World, Trans International, Arrow Air, Rich and Overseas National. They all came to Gatwick. Saturn switched from DC-7Cs to operate five DC-8s from 1967; two series 50s and three stretched 'Combi' Series 61s. Flights to Europe were flown from JFK in New York. In 1976, Saturn was bought out by the Transamerica Corp and was absorbed into Trans International Airlines that December, making TIA the largest non-scheduled airline in the world. (John Mounce)

▲ On final approach to Runway 27 at Gatwick in February 1969, British United's BAC 1-11 Series 201AC G-ASJD was the sixth One-Eleven to fly. The much-loved sandstone and blue colour scheme looked good on all BUA aircraft and the company's very smart air hostess uniforms were made in the same colour blue. Apart from domestic destinations, in 1969, BUA's 1-11s could be spied all over Western Europe including Malaga, Palma, Gibraltar, Lisbon, Madrid, Amsterdam, Rotterdam, Genoa and Paris. Before delivery to BUA, G-ASJD was specially modified with a powered elevator, a large tail parachute, modified reverse thrust actuators and a modified wing leading edge to take on stalling tests. During these tests it was damaged in a crash-landing on Salisbury Plain in August 1964. After a rebuild, it was delivered to Gatwick from Wisley on 5 August 1965 and later carried both Caledonian//BUA and British Caledonian titles. From 1971 it flew with the Royal Aircraft Establishment as XX105 and was eventually scrapped in 2012. (Author's collection)

➤ The first BUA aircraft to receive this very smart sandstone and blue scheme was VC10 G-ASIX in August 1966. The repaint from the old-fashioned dark blue cheatline took seven days and 30 gallons of paint. Under Freddie Laker's leadership, BUA ordered two new VC10s in 1961. The first two (G-ASIX and G-ASIW) were delivered in September/October 1964 and both had large freight doors in the forward fuselage. Because of the growth in BUA's South American traffic, a third new VC10 (G-ATDJ) was bought from BAC after its buyer, Ghana Airways, cancelled their order. G-ARTA, seen here at the end of the South Pier in September 1969, was the very first VC10 built and became the fourth of its type to join the BUA fleet in 1969 after completing test flying and a spell under lease to Middle East Airlines. Its demise at Gatwick in 1972 in the hands of British Caledonian is recorded on another page. (Pete Waterfield)

▲ Nice early shot of Trans International's Douglas DC-8-55F N3325T taken on 24 July 1966 on a charter from the USA complete with a Dan-Air Ambassador parked up behind it. Note the title 'DC-8F Fan Jet Trader', showing that this version could be used for freighting thanks to its forward port-side main-deck freight door. TIA received its first jetliner, a DC-8, in November 1962 with N3325T being delivered brand new in May 1965; it left the fleet in 1970. From 1968, TIA was owned by the giant Transamerica Corporation, which was based in San Francisco. The airline was merged with Saturn Airways (another old Gatwick airline) in 1976. The name was changed again in 1979 to Transamerica Airlines and its fleet of DC-8s, DC-10s and Boeing 747s were used on schedules to Shannon and Amsterdam, with some appearing at Gatwick on charters. (Author's collection)

▲ More usually seen on schedules from Casablanca to Heathrow, Royal Air Maroc (RAM) Caravelles first appeared at Gatwick with a summertime series of Sunday flights from Tangier in 1967. Caravelle III CN-CCY waits for its passengers on the south finger on 24 September 1967 with BEA Viscount G-APEX behind. Delivered in 1963, she was one of five Caravelles operated by the airline up until 1976/77. RAM has had a long association with Gatwick and still visits using Boeing 737s. Its rather classy 1960s livery has barely been altered up to this day. The £500,000 administration block on top of the original (South) terminal can be seen taking shape in the background of this picture. Finished in 1972, it was an additional five storeys above the terminal and the top floor contained the Airport Authority's Ground Operations, which had been moved from the centre finger. The small 'box' sticking out from the terminal roof was the Ground Movement Control room manned by ATC staff. Note the crowds of spectators enjoying a day out in the sun on the viewing deck. (Terry Rattue)

◄ The first jetliners to use Gatwick were mostly diversion arrivals from Heathrow in the early 1960s. However, there were some interesting charters by BOAC in the summer of 1962 that definitely brought in some big jets. The UK government was concerned about the number of black immigrants arriving from the Commonwealth countries in the West Indies and passed the Commonwealth Immigrants Act (1962). Prior to this Act coming into force on 1 July 1962, BOAC operated at least sixteen charters into Gatwick using Boeing 707s up to 27 June. BOAC archives show that G-ARRA was the preferred aircraft, although G-APFB, seen here, is listed as inbound on 1 May. (Author's collection)

➤ Malaysia-Singapore Airlines (MSA) Comet 9V-BAT arrived at Gatwick on 31 August 1969 on delivery to Dan-Air. The latter bought seven Comet 4s from MSA in 1969 and at least six of them – 9V-BAS/BAT/BAU/G-APDP (was 9V-BBH) and 9M-AOB/AOD – transited through Gatwick prior to positioning to Lasham for overhaul and repaint. This Comet 4 had previously served with BOAC from October 1958 as G-APDC. After overhaul, it again became G-APDC with Dan-Air and remained in service until 10 April 1973, after which it was ferried to Lasham and scrapped. Dan-Air's search for cheap Comets worldwide was successful, with examples appearing from Argentina, Egypt, Sudan and Kuwait. In total Dan-Air owned forty-nine different examples, although not all of them were flown in service. (Bob Wall collection)

◀ In the author's view, the short-fuselage Douglas DC-9s were much prettier than the stretched MD-82s etc. This very nice DC-9-15 shows off its previous owner Swissair's colours while taxying inbound on 4 August 1969 past a selection of 'Tiddlers' parked on the grass behind. D-AMOR was leased from April 1969 and, because of the French language 'Amor' in the registration, it was given the name 'Lovebird' on the port side only. It returned to Douglas off lease in August after only four months' service. Germanair was originally called Sudwestflug and after the DC-9 left, it obtained its first BAC 1-11 in October 1969. It later flew Fokker 28s and A300s, and in 1977 became Bavaria/Germanair after the airlines merged. (Christian Volpati collection)

▶ Yes I know the line-up in the background is pretty impressive but this Eastern Air Lines Boeing 720-025 N8708E is a real rarity at Gatwick. It arrived from Basle on 16 October 1969 at 0959 as EA7401 and night-stopped before departing to Shannon for a fuel stop en route to the USA at 1044 on the 17th using the same flight number. A few days after this flight, Eastern traded it into Boeing in a part-exchange deal involving Boeing 727-225s. Boeing eventually sold N8708E to a leasing company, which leased it to Calair in Germany. (David Freeman)

➤ The worst aviation accident ever to occur at Gatwick was back in January 1969. This Ariana Afghan Airlines Boeing 727-113C with sixty-two passengers and crew on board was completing its schedule from Kabul to London via Kandahar, Beirut, Istanbul and Frankfurt. In thick fog and total darkness at 1.30 in the morning, flight 701 was established and descending on the ILS to Runway 27 when the pilot was distracted by a stabiliser warning light and allowed the aircraft to descend below the glide path. The aircraft hit tree tops before rolling right and smashing into a house 1.5 miles from the threshold. Forty-eight passengers and crew were killed along with two occupants of the house. (Jacques Guillem Collection)

◄ An interesting visitor on 25 September 1968 was this seventy-four-seater BAC 1-11 420EL registered in Argentina as LV-JGX. Passing through on its delivery flight from Hurn, then to Argentina via Keflavik on the 26th, it was delivered to Aerotransportes Litoral Argentino, S.A. (ALA), which was based at Buenos Aires-Aeroparque. ALA was 30 per cent owned by Austral, which later became the largest operator of 1-11s in South America. It ordered four Series 420ELs for both Austral and ALA with options for a pair of Series 500s in May 1967. Austral and ALA formally merged in June 1971, and between them they flew fourteen 1-11s, both owned and leased. The front fuselage of LV-JGX was badly damaged by an oxygen fire on the ground in January 1978 but the nose from another 1-11 was later grafted on and it was still flying in the USA in the late 1980s. (Jacques Guillem collection)

▲ Few jet airliners could be identified so easily on final approach as a Coronado. The four General Electric CJ805-23 turbofans were so smoky, it was obvious to an observer just what type was about to grace the ramp at Gatwick. Modern Air Transport was a US-based non-scheduled and supplemental carrier that found a niche market in West Berlin flying tourists on IT charters. It bought five CV990As from American Airlines – airline boss Mort Beyer said 'cheap to buy … expensive to fly' – in 1967 and commenced operations in March 1968. At the time they were the world's fastest airliners (621mph max), like Nordair Canada, but Modern flew them at reduced speeds in order to reduce its fuel bill. Although passengers were squeezed into narrow seats to increase the capacity from 125 to 149, the type was popular and by 1972 Modern had eight in service. All of them visited Gatwick until Modern shut down the Berlin business in 1974; sometimes there were several parked up in a neat line. In this March 1969 shot, note the famous anti-shock fairings/fuel tanks above the trailing edge that were sometimes called Küchemann carrots! (Author's collection)

◄ Canadian Pacific Air Lines (CPAL) had been visiting Gatwick for ages with Bristol Britannias but it was able to upgrade to pure jets for the summer 1965 season using DC-8-40s. Later in the 1960s, competition for the CPAL charters hotted up with the arrival of Wardair with new Boeing 707-300s and Pacific Western with ex-Qantas Boeing 707-100s. CPAL, which from 1968 had rebranded as CP Air, countered by moving up the Gatwick route to DC-8-60s in 1969. These visits were never in the airline's timetables as they were always charters. The first ever CPAL Douglas DC-8 service was from Vancouver to Honolulu in March 1961. This is DC-8-43 CF-CPJ *Empress of Toronto*, which first appeared at LGW in July 1965. (Tim Spearman collection)

2

THE SEVENTIES

The year 1970 was when Gatwick saw BEA Airtours upgrade its fleet with Comets. Dan-Air's Comets were already well established at their home airport and although none of these fleets were new, these over-powered and noisy jetliners became synonymous with the airport that by 1977 boasted three piers (the centre pier having been renovated with moving walkways and air bridges) and a new cargo area. Spectators were initially still encouraged to visit from 8 a.m. until dusk with entry to the viewing decks by lifts from the International Arrivals Concourse, but due to 'heightened security' measures they were closed in 1973. A 1975 brochure highlighting the 'New Gatwick' gave a list of the airlines that could be seen regularly on charters or schedules: Air Malawi, Britannia, British Airtours, British Caledonian, British Island Airways, British Midland, Dan-Air, Laker, NLM, ONA, SAM, Wardair and World Airways. Many of them are illustrated in the following pages but sadly none of them still exist.

▲ Set up in 1965 by Thai Royal family member Prince Varanand as Varan Air-Siam, it wasn't until 1969 that Air Siam acquired its first aircraft, a trio of Douglas DC-4s from Australia. Its first leased Boeing 707, HS-VGA 'Chao Phraya', arrived in October 1972 but was returned to Israel in September 1973 and replaced by HS-VGC 'Pahsak', which is seen here on its delivery flight through Gatwick on 26 September 1973. Air Siam's April 1974 timetable shows it was flying thrice-weekly schedules from Bangkok to Tokyo via Hong Kong and then the flight carried on to Honolulu and Los Angeles by Continental DC-10. This low-cost service became very popular but was only so due to massive ticket discounting. The airline leased an A300, a DC-10 and a B747 but its accounts were a mess, with one commentator accusing the company of 'political wire pulling, extensive fare cutting and financial sleight of hand'. The Thai authorities, which had always sided with Thai International, withdrew its licence on 4 February 1977. (Bernard King)

◄ Initially formed in 1945 as Riddle Airlines, Airlift International operated charter flights until 1956, when it commenced scheduled services. In 1968 it acquired cargo operator Slick Airways and from its Miami base flew to the mainland USA, the Caribbean and South America. Airlift acquired its first of four 707s (N737AL) on lease in 1967. The illustrated N739AL arrived at LGW on 2 July 1970 for a sub-lease to Caledonian for transatlantic services for a few days prior to the arrival of G-ATZC (ex N737AL) on delivery to Caledonian on the 7th. N739AL returned to Airlift in New York the next day and in 1971 was leased to Aerolineas Argentinas. Financial problems forced Airlift to file for Chapter 11 protection in mid 1981 and despite reorganising and refinancing a couple of times, its final bankruptcy was declared in 1991. (Tony Eastwood collection)

◄ BEA Airtours received nine 109-seater De Havilland Comet 4Bs from BEA stocks and made its first IT service from Gatwick to Palma on 6 March 1970. The airline took over the old Air Couriers hangar that had been used by Transglobe prior to its demise. In this picture, the huge 'barn door' flaps on Comet 4B G-ARGM are set to 'full flap' (80 degrees) to slow the 11-year-old jet to 120 knots for landing on runway 26 in July 1973. The last Airtours Comet service was on 31 October 1973, leaving the airline with a fleet of similarly ageing and audible ex-BOAC Rolls-Royce Conway-powered Boeing 707-436 airliners. G-ARGM was sold to Dan-Air London the following month but was only used for spares. (Author's collection)

▲ Series 509EW BAC 1-11 G-AWWX made its first flight from Bournemouth Hurn airport on 11 February 1969 and, as usual for Caledonian Airways, it was given a name, in this case 'Flagship Isle of Skye'. Delivered to Gatwick the following month, it only stayed with these titles until late 1970, when Caledonian merged with BUA. Bought by Dan-Air London in 1975, it remained based at Gatwick until 1992, when it was sold to British Air Ferries. After a ferry flight to Southend from Hurn it never entered service but remained stored there, despite an unfulfilled sale to Nigeria, until it was scrapped in September 1998. BAF (later British World Airlines) operated a total of seven BAC 1-11s, and many of them visited LGW. Note the pair of Douglas DC-7 propliners from Aer Turas and Dan-Air parked on the South Park. (Stephen Wolf)

◄ Singapore's first private airline, Saber Air, was founded in 1966 with a fleet of C-47 Dakotas, Twin Otters and several Cessnas and Pipers, operating mostly charter flights for the oil industry in Southeast Asia. In 1969, the Singapore government took over 80 per cent of the shares in Saber Air in an attempt to control the civil aviation industry there. From 1970, Saber flew with a DC-3 and a pair of DC-6s, but in 1971 it started Singapore–London (Gatwick) ad hoc charters with this DC-8-61 9V-BEH on lease (for $89,500 per month) from US-based Trans International Airlines. However, the relationship between TIA and Saber did not last long, possibly because the DC-8 was always breaking down! It was returned to TIA in 1973 and replaced with a Boeing 707 leased from BCal. (Author's collection)

▲ Channel Airways Vickers Viscounts were a regular sight at Gatwick but Channel's jetliners (Comets, Tridents and 1-11s) were certainly not, appearing a handful of times in the late 1960s and early '70s, some of them diversions from Stansted where Channel kept its jetliners. The appearance of the 109-seater Channel DH Comets at Gatwick was also related to their use by Gatwick-based BEA Airtours. About once a week in the summer of 1970, a Channel Comet would position to Gatwick from Stansted to fly one or two services for Airtours and then return to Stansted the next day. Channel's DH Dove G-ANVU would act as a crew transfer when required. Seen here on 4 September 1971 is Comet 4B G-APYD, which first flew for Channel in April 1970. Note the very basic BEA colours and the Donaldson 707 inbound behind it. (Peter Marson)

▲ The reliable old DC-6 propliners of Alitalia's charter arm Società Aerea Mediterranea (SAM) were retired in 1968 and replaced by a fleet of Caravelles for charters around Europe including Gatwick. Seven different Caravelles were leased long-term to SAM from Alitalia, however Alitalia Caravelles also appeared at Gatwick in full Alitalia colours, sometimes carrying 'Chartered by SAM' stickers. This is Caravelle VI-N I-DABP 'Castore' in March 1972 carrying the original Alitalia-style cheat line, which was modified for SAM by changing the thicker blue lines to red. SAM's finances suffered in 1972 and parent company Alitalia decided to wind down its charter arm and merge all the charter operations under one roof. SAM flew its last Caravelle service in 1977. (Jacques Guillem collection)

◄ Interesting view on 1 June 1973 looking west from the spectators' deck with Iberia's 1961-vintage Douglas DC-8-52 EC-ARB taking centre stage accompanied by a pair of BEA Airtours Comets, two BEA Airtours 707s, a Wardair 707, a BCal 707, an ONA DC-10 and a Capitol DC-8. This visit may well have been a diversion of the scheduled flight to Heathrow as that day thirty-two aircraft diverted to Gatwick from Heathrow. Similar numbers diverted the previous two days, too. EC-ARB made many flights on Aviaco charters in full Iberia colours, with the first one logged on 30 August 1970 from and to Palma. After it was bought outright by Aviaco, it was repainted in Aviaco's tasteful gold/red colours and then after 1974 in its blue/white colour scheme. The airline's best year was in 1982 when it carried an impressive 2.1 million passengers. Aviaco flew fifteen different DC-8s, including five 'stretched' DC-8s in the 1980s. (Ian Anderson)

➤ British Midland Airways (BMA) leased this Boeing 707-321 G-AYBJ to the Israeli national airline EL AL for short periods in 1970 and 1971 and for a couple of months in the summer of 1972. The Gatwick logs show that it had first visited Gatwick on EL AL charters in 1970, probably in these BMA colours with EL AL titles. Over the next ten years 'Bravo Juliet' was leased to a huge number of operators worldwide including Iraqi, Syrian Arab and Pakistan International. EL AL had first used a Boeing 707 for its New York schedules in 1961 when it leased one from VARIG. Later that year it bought its own 707s and then in 1962 acquired a pair of Boeing 720s. This airframe survived until 1988, when it was scrapped at Sharjah. (Jacques Guillem collection)

Luton-based Autair International operated a fleet of five BAC 1-11 series 518s from December 1969. After the rebranding into Court Line in January 1970, the 1-11s were repainted into some very colourful schemes, reportedly to get the inclusive tour (IT) holidaymakers into a sunny mood prior to arriving at their resort. The airline flew for Horizon Holidays but its largest customer was the giant tour operator Clarksons, whose logo 'C' was applied to the fin. Eleven different Court Line 1-11s visited LGW, starting in the summer of 1970. After a big downturn in traffic caused by the Arab–Israeli war, which led to fuel price hikes, and with a huge bill for the purchase of a pair of TriStars (both of them visiting Gatwick), Court Line collapsed in August 1974. (Stephen Wolf)

Now here is a real rarity at Gatwick on 18 May 1972. Laker's BAC 1-11 G-AVBY was given these special titles as part of a publicity event by the giant chemical company Du Pont, which made, amongst other items, ladies' underwear and nylon stockings. The idea was a contest to find a young woman who could be featured in the Du Pont magazine adverts under the strap line 'The most wanted woman on earth'. The winners were lavished with prizes including cash, a car, a cruise and holidays abroad. The competition appears to have lasted a few years but no other aeronautical connections have been found. G-AVBY probably made a few special flights in connection with the competition. (Jonathan Walton)

◄ Mey-Air Transport A/S was set up by shipping magnate Hans Meyer in 1969 using some small twin-props plus a Convair 240 bought from Polaris Air Transport for ad hoc and IT charters from its initial base at Oslo-Gardermoen. Mey-Air also bought a NAMC YS-11A in late 1970; this flew to Gatwick in July 1971 but it lasted less than a year. The Convair was retired in 1973, leaving services to be flown by a pair of new Boeing 737-200s that had joined the fleet in 1971. They were flown on IT flights from Norway and Sweden but they were rarely seen at Gatwick. LN-MTC, seen here in May 1973, first visited Gatwick in December 1971; the other was LN-MTD, which also appeared late in 1971. Both were repossessed by Boeing after Mey-Air collapsed in February 1974 when the 1973 oil crisis hit the IT market. A Mey-Air Boeing 737 featured strongly in the Sean Connery movie *Ransom* in 1974. (Caz Caswell)

► Balair's Douglas DC-9 series 33CF HB-IDN was delivered new to Switzerland in April 1970, so it was only a month old when seen here at Gatwick on a charter flight from Zurich. With a history going back to 1925, Balair had first appeared at Gatwick with its Vickers Vikings and DC-4s in 1959. Even after it had switched to pure jet aircraft, Balair continued famously to operate Douglas DC-6 HB-IBS into Gatwick on regular charters until October 1981. HB-IDN passed to Itavia in 1977 and continued to visit Gatwick in its colours for a few more years. (Robin Ridley)

➤ West German charter airline Bavaria Fluggesellschaft was founded in 1957 with a single Piper Apache used for air taxi work. By 1964, Bavaria was flying Dart Heralds on holiday charters, and by 1970, the last Herald had left the fleet and Bavaria became an all BAC 1-11 airline with several IT services flown out of Gatwick to Germany. Each 1-11 was inscribed 'Holiday Jet' on the engines and was given a registration that made a word in English, such as D-ANDY, D-AILY, D-AISY and D-ANNO. This is D-AISY, named 'Dominikus Zimmermann' after the German Rococo architect and stuccoist – no, I don't know what that is either. In March 1977, Bavaria merged with rival Germanair and the new grouping became the unimaginatively named Bavaria-Germanair. (Bob Wall)

▲ The visit of Air Liberia's Boeing 737-2Q5C to Gatwick in 1979 was a nice surprise for the aircraft enthusiasts. EL-AIL was the only Boeing 737 registered in the UK and the brand new 1978 aircraft was delivered via Amsterdam to Monrovia. Despite the airline livery, it appears that it was mostly used for VIP and government flights.

In 1979, it was seen at various airports in Europe including London Stansted. It was sold in the Congo in 1982. This was not the only Liberian-registered jet airliner to appear at Gatwick; various freighter 707s have visited as well as a TriStar, a DC-8, a Boeing 727 and even a Yak-40. (Author)

▼ The first visit to LGW by Aeroflot's finest jetliner occurred on Sunday, 4 July 1965 when Tupolev Tu-104B CCCP-42507 arrived from Leningrad. By the early 1970s, the regular weekend package holiday services from the Russian city were all flown by the Tu-104, often with two arriving each Saturday morning. If the runway was wet or snowy and you were very lucky, you may have seen them use their two tail parachutes for additional braking (they had no reverse thrust). No fun for the BAA Operations man who had to retrieve them and a nightmare if the chutes were dropped on the runway. Shrouded in mystery until it first appeared in the West in 1956, the 104 was the Soviets' first jet airliner. Its wings, tailplane, fin, landing gear, cockpit equipment and engines were based on the Tu-16 medium-range bomber but it had a new-build, 3.2m-diameter fuselage. The prototype Tu-104 was built in Moscow and made its first flight in June 1955, two years earlier than the Western rival Boeing 707 and DH Comet 4. More than thirty-five different Tu-104s visited LGW, all of them Aeroflot. (Peter Guiver)

▲ Despite being a British-built airliner, the Trident was never a common sight at Gatwick but when fog struck Heathrow then the occasional one diverted in. Additionally, new Tridents on test flights out of Hatfield appeared for Instrument Landing System (ILS) approaches and circuits. Not well known is the fact that British Airways Trident 2s flew schedules to Spain from Gatwick in summer 1980, replacing 737s. British European Airways' Trident 3 G-AWZD is seen taxying inbound sometime in 1972; note the fourth engine at the base of the rudder. The power from the three RR Spey 512 engines was not enough for the heavyweight Trident 3 (that's why Tridents were called ground grippers!), so an RB162 booster engine was fitted to provide an additional 5,250lb of thrust during take-off and climb-out. BEA never wanted the Trident 3; it wanted Boeing 727s but was refused permission to buy them. In 1968 it said, 'The Trident 3 is an excellent aircraft from the passenger's point of view, but basically too small for BEA's needs.' (Caz Caswell)

◄ Thanks to lack of encouragement by the British Labour government for a merger between ailing BUA and a strong Caledonian Airways in 1969, BUA nearly had the joy of being bought out by BOAC. However, a U-turn by the government brought some fresh thinking about a 'Second Force' airline, allowing Caledonian Airways to buy British United Airways for £6.9 million in late 1970. The resulting airline was initially named Caledonian//BUA (note the double slash between the names) and continued operations with a fleet of thirty-one jetliners (707s, VC10s and BAC 1-11s) and a staff of 4,400. This unruly airline name was short-lived as boss Adam Thompson announced to a press conference in September 1971 that the new name would be British Caledonian Airways and it would be referred to as BCal. Delivered new to BUA in 1965, G-ASJI was actually the very first 1-11 to be handed to its customer after type certification was completed. It remained Gatwick-based until sold to Pacific Express as N106EX in 1982. (Author's collection)

➤ Tracing its history way back to 1948, US charter airline World Airways made its fortune by operating passenger and freight flights for the US Government, starting with the Korean War and continuing with other conflicts that the USA was involved in. World Airways became the USA's first charter carrier to buy jetliners when it ordered three Boeing 707s in May 1962. Douglas DC-8-63CFs were added to the fleet from 1971 and its last 707 (they operated thirteen in total) was disposed of in 1977. Boeing 707-373C N369WA is seen here displaying a full set of landing flaps and spoilers rolling out after arriving on a transatlantic charter in August 1971. Five years later it flew into a mountain near Tehran while owned by Korean Airlines. (Author's collection)

◄ In order to compete with Air France's Caravelles on the Tunis to Paris schedule, Tunis Air bought a single Caravelle III, TS-IKM, in 1961. As the network increased, three more examples were acquired in the mid 1960s, including Caravelle III TS-MAC seen here in 1971. Much larger Boeing 727s joined the fleet from 1971 but traffic peaks saw Tunis Air leasing more Caravelles during the early 1970s with examples from Sabena, Transavia, Sterling and Trans-Union. Eventually the 727s replaced the Caravelles, with the last three retiring in 1977. (John Mounce)

▲ Originally a Danish charter operator with Fokker Friendships, Maersk Air bought a couple of major tour operators in 1971 and planned to enter the IT charter market. To this end, it acquired three ex-Northwest Airlines Boeing 720Bs and made the first 720B service from Copenhagen to Rhodes in March 1973. Two more were acquired and the type was very successful with the airline, even operating transatlantic charters to the USA and Canada from 1976. The airline's all-over pale blue colour scheme was a familiar sight at Gatwick right up until the type was removed from the fleet in 1987. (Author's collection)

◄ JAT (Jugoslovenski Aerotransport) Sud Aviation Caravelle VI-N, YU-AHA 'Dubrovnik' first appeared at Gatwick in July 1966 and is seen here in her last summer season ten years later in April 1976. The aircraft was delivered to JAT in 1963, the first of eight of its type to serve with the airline. JAT often operated charter services in Europe using 'JR' flight prefixes in addition to the carrier's scheduled routes (JU prefix) flown as the Yugoslavian national airline. Gatwick had first seen the JAT colours way back in 1962 when DC-3 YU-ACB arrived. The presence of a JAT Boeing 727 behind suggests their visits are associated with the late Easter holiday period of that year. The JAT Caravelle fleet made good money for the airline and was retired in 1976. (John Crawford)

▲ British Caledonian's beautiful VC10 G-ARTA (it was the prototype VC10) had been diverted to Heathrow due to fog at Gatwick. Before daylight the next day, 28 January 1972, it departed LHR with just four aboard for the short hop back to Gatwick at the usual altitude for a LHR–LGW trip of 2,000ft – I bet that woke up a few people! It was vectored for an ILS approach to runway 08 in quite blustery conditions and the captain elected to keep a higher speed than usual due to the wind gusts. On landing, it all went terribly wrong; the aircraft hit the runway hard and spoilers and reverse thrust were selected but it bounced up and came down again nose wheel first, followed by two more bounces before coming to a stop. The third contact with the ground was later measured at 3.55G. Despite the VC10's strength, it was badly damaged with creases in the fuselage fore and aft of the wings, a broken nose undercarriage and a broken main gear axle. The aircraft was used as a source of spare parts for the next two years before being chopped up. BCal apprentice engineers used bits of the fuselage to make souvenir plaques to fund-raise for the Golden Lion Children's Trust. (Dave Freeman)

▲ Without doubt, the only image in this book taken out of the window of an Aeroflot Tupolev Tu-104 is this one of Alitalia Caravelle VIN I-DABG 'Arturo' in September 1975. Quite how the photographer managed to get this shot is unknown but the author is both impressed and grateful. Note the ever continuing work on the South Terminal and the last three digits of the Tu-104's registration CCCP-42419 on top of the wing. Alitalia commenced Caravelle operations in June 1960 and its charter arm Societa Aerea Mediterranea often used them from 1968 onwards. This one carries 'Chartered by SAM' titles, while some had full SAM titles. SAM was eventually merged into Alitalia in 1974 and ceased to exist in 1977. (Author's collection)

◄ About to taxi out for Runway 26 at Gatwick in October 1973 is the colourful DC-8-21 EC-CAM of Palma-based charter airline Air Spain. One of six DC-8s in its fleet that replaced the four Bristol Britannias that were also regulars at LGW from 1967, EC-CAM 'Isla de Ibiza' had been acquired from Eastern Air Lines. Operating these fuel thirsty DC-8s was not good for the company's economics and after some unsuccessful merger talks with Aviaco in early 1975, the airline shut down and the DC-8 fleet was put into store, with EC-CAM being parked at Gran Canaria. It was repossessed by Eastern the following year, flown to Marana and eventually broken up in 1978. (Author's collection)

◄ An iconic shot of Dan-Air's BAC 1-11 G-AXCP on Stand 1 at Gatwick in August 1972 with a ground engineer in his oil-stained white overalls chatting to a Dan-Air hostie while the Customs and Excise man is in the cockpit to check the ship's papers, leaving his trusty 1970 1098cc Morris Minor four-door saloon at the bottom of the airstairs. This BAC 1-11, built four years before the Morris Minor, was a Series 401AK built for American Airlines. Dan-Air had it from 1969 until 1986, when it went to Florida Express in the USA. Remarkably, this old lady was still airworthy in 2017 – one of two ex-Dan-Air BAC 1-11s used as flying test beds by Northrop Grumman Systems Corp based at Baltimore/Washington International Thurgood Marshall Airport. N162W (ex-G-AXCP) was finally retired in late 2017, while N164W (ex-G-AXCK) remained as the last flying 1-11 until 2019. (Author's collection)

◄ Transportes Aéreos Portugueses (TAP) got its first three Caravelle VI-Rs in 1962 for European trunk routes. In 1968 it leased a final Caravelle from Cruzeiro just to cover the busy summer season. This is TAP's first Caravelle, CS-TCA 'Goa', which made its first visit to Gatwick as TP450 on 4 December 1962 on a diversion from Heathrow. It reappeared on another Heathrow diversion the following January. The fleet was sold in 1975 to SAN Ecuador and this one was last seen derelict in Ecuador in 1994. (Author's collection)

◄ In the summer of 1979, British Airtours operated its Boeing 707-436 G-APFD in this hybrid colour scheme. The airline had wet-leased the 707 to Air Mauritius for its long-haul international services in October 1977 and the aircraft had been painted in Airtours' stunning red and white scheme. When it returned off lease after Air Mauritius bought its own B707-320Bs, Airtours decided not to fully repaint the aircraft but just re-did the fin and left the Air Mauritius cheat line. At the end of the summer 1979 season it was sold back to Boeing and it later operated in the USA until it was grounded in 1986. (Tony Hyatt)

➤ This airline dates back to 1948 when Aviaco (Aviación y Comercio S.A.) was formed in Bilbao to operate both domestic and international services with six Bristol Freighters. In 1954, the national airline of Spain, Iberia, bought 33 per cent of the company and thereby formed a good working relationship between the two. From 1960, Aviaco operated to Gatwick using Convairliners, then from 1963 DC-4s and DC-6s. From 1969, Aviaco flew IT services to Gatwick using Iberia Caravelles. In the early 1980s, Aviaco acquired a fleet of stretched DC-8s that Iberia no longer required, but before that it had about ten Series 50 DC-8s, including EC-ATP that wore this attractive gold and red scheme. EC-ATP went to the Spanish Air Force in 1980. (Author's collection)

△ Starting with three Gatwick-based Bristol Britannias in 1969 for summer holiday charters, Donaldson International Airways bought a pair of Boeing 707-321s (G-AYVG and this one, G-AYXR) from Pan Am in December 1970 for transatlantic charters. Two more ex-Pan Am 707s arrived in November 1971, and in late 1972 one of them flew a weekly Gatwick to Dhaka service on behalf of Bangladesh Biman. Donaldson became one of the airlines to get involved with the affinity charters controversy, which upset the US authorities. In addition, the British CAA demanded Donaldson increase its capital, which made it sell a couple of 707s, but it managed to get them back later. In May 1974 Donaldson leased two (later three) 707s to Iraqi Airways for use on its international schedules. Donaldson stopped flying on 8 August 1974 and its remaining 707s were repossessed by Pan Am and returned to Miami. G-AYXR, here parked up in April 1974, carries the name 'Snared'. (John Crawford)

◄ One of the twenty Boeing 727s operated by Dan-Air London to replace its DH Comets, G-BFGM was bought from the USA and arrived at Gatwick on Christmas Eve in 1977. This 727-95 was built in 1966 for Northeast Airlines (the US version) and served with Dan-Air until December 1982. Dan-Air were the first British airline to operate the 727, reconfiguring its fleet at its Lasham maintenance base with 150 seats instead of the original 131 and commencing services in the spring of 1973 for Clarksons, Global and Lunn Poly. Cockpit crews for Dan-Air's B727s were trained on a simulator housed in Horsham, the author's home town. (Author)

➤ Initially set up in 1969 under the name Società Aerea Veneziana (SAV) in Venice, Italian charter airline Aeropa flew two Boeing 707s: this -321C N716HH leased from Pan Ayer and -131 I-SAVA, which was leased from Israeli Aircraft Industries from September 1972. Before any flights could happen, SAV was restructured due to delays by the Italian authorities and I-SAVA was sub-leased to the new airline Aeropa in 1973. Operations started in the summer of 1973, with I-SAVA appearing at Gatwick that November. N716HH was painted at Stansted in 1974 and appeared at Gatwick in July that year. These old 707s suffered many technical and corrosion problems, causing long delays, and with the airline struggling financially, operations were wound up in early 1975 after N716HH had made its last flight Gatwick–Heathrow–Stansted on 31 January 1975. Its remnants were still on the Stansted fire dump in 1981. (Geoff Dobson)

▲ Air Malta was set up by the Maltese government in 1973 with support from Pakistan International Airlines, which leased Boeing 720s to Air Malta in 1974. As with many new carriers, plans for new routes and schedules ran ahead of aircraft procurement, particularly in the busy summer months. Therefore BAC 1-11-530FX G-AYOP was leased from BCal between April and October 1975 in this semi-disguised BCal colour scheme. G-AYOP had Gatwick associations from its earliest days, first appearing in the pastel yellow of Court Line in April 1971.

After the airline's demise, it was acquired by BCal and then later subsumed into the British Airways fleet when BA took over the much loved 'Cally' in 1988. When BA disposed of its 1-11 fleet in the early 1990s, it found a new lease of life among the large number acquired by Bournemouth-based European Aviation and once again it became a regular sight at Gatwick, often on sub-charter work. It was updated with a Rockwell Collins flight deck and in the late 1990s was leased to Luton-based Debonair, which also flew it to Gatwick. (Caz Caswell)

➤ This rather yucky colour scheme belongs to German charter airline Aviaction. Formed in Hamburg in 1969, it competed with Atlantis, Bavaria, Condor and LTU. It chose the sixty-five-seat Fokker F28 Fellowship as it could land at smaller southern European airports and the first one (D-AHLA seen here) was delivered in February 1971 and made its first service to Palma that March. Two more F28s arrived that year and all three made visits to LGW in the summer of 1972. By 1973 the airline was looking for investors to expand operations; sadly this never happened and after suffering financial problems it was forced to shut down in late 1973. (Keith Brooks)

▲ Britannia Airways had to seek out larger types when it decided to enter the potentially huge affinity group US charter business in 1971. This was a way of circumnavigating the regulated minimum International Air Transport Association (IATA) fares by allowing 'groups' or 'clubs' to charter an aircraft to travel. The whole thing was a sham as many passengers 'joined' a totally fake club before travelling to Europe mainly from the West Coast of the USA. Britannia, which had eight Boeing 737s at this time, leased this six-abreast 189-seater Boeing 707 G-AYSI from World Airways for $6 million and another (G-AYEX) later from Executive Jet Aviation. Britannia's 707s were also used for freight services from Heathrow to Nairobi for Simbair and taking racehorses to Japan. The affinity group game was scrapped and replaced in 1973 with much better-regulated 'advanced passenger charters' (ABC), which initially required passengers to book four weeks in advance. Britannia disposed of the two 707s to British Caledonian. (Author's collection)

▲ Starting with two ex-Swissair Convair 440s in 1969, Zagreb-based Pan Adria flew regional scheduled passenger services but struggled to compete against the government-supported JAT Airways. Pan Adria bought two more Convairliners and five Fairchild FH-227s, one of which was written off at Zagreb in 1977. Its only jetliners were a Boeing 727 and this DC-9-32 YU-AJF, which was acquired in May 1973 and passed to Inex Adria in April 1974. In December 1978 the Yugoslav government took control of Pan Adria and the company was renamed Trans Adria Airways. In the 1980s, this DC-9 flew for British Midland as G-BMWD. (Andy Marsh)

◀ Tracing its origins back to a small mining support outfit owned by Max Ward in 1946, Wardair was formed in 1952 and commenced ops with a DHC-3 Otter in June 1953. Transatlantic charters started in 1962 with DC-6B CF-PCI leased from Canadian Pacific, which did visit Gatwick. From 1966, Wardair flights to Gatwick used a Boeing 727-100 CF-FUN and, once the DC-6s had been retired, the airline bought a pair of Boeing 707-320Cs, CF-FAN and the illustrated CF-ZYP 'W.R. Wop May', which first appeared on 30 March 1969. As the airline grew, the 707s were replaced by 747s and DC-10s. Wardair was absorbed into Canadian Airlines International in October 1989 and CF-ZYP survived to join the United States Air Force in 1985. (Author's collection)

◄ Dan-Air London's three ex-Japan Air Lines Boeing 727-100s were the first to be granted a British Certificate of Airworthiness. In order to achieve this, the company had to spend an absolute fortune to modify the aircraft and this shot of G-BAEF at Gatwick in March 1973 shows just how much bodywork Boeing engineers in the USA had to do to add an extra emergency exit to cope with the 150 passengers. In addition, a full stall protection system costing around £100,000 per aircraft was designed and fitted, consisting of a stick pusher, a stick nudger and an independent stick shaker for each pilot. Dan-Air went on to own twenty Boeing 727s, including the stretched Series 200, into which it squeezed 189 punters. (Author's collection)

▲ Laker Airways Boeing 707-138 G-AVZZ spent a good deal of its time with Laker with the International Caribbean Airways titling and Barbados flag seen here in 1971. Operating schedules between Barbados and Luxembourg via Gatwick, International Caribbean was owned by the Barbados government (51 per cent) and Laker Airways. It was designated the island's national carrier in 1975 and this 707 operated with the company until 1978, briefly returning to Laker before sale. An early production 707, G-AVZZ began life with Qantas back in 1959, and was acquired by British Eagle International Airlines in 1968 as part of Eagle's second challenge to BOAC's Western Atlantic operations, initially serving Bermuda. Sadly, Eagle suffered financial failure due to a combination of factors that year, ironically making G-AVZZ available to Laker, who would use her for a similar operation. Equally ironic is that Laker, rather than Harold Bamberg's Eagle, is commonly seen as the godfather of the British independents. (Author's collection)

▼ From summer 1971, BCal's 'Africargo' freight to East and Central Africa was carried in this dedicated Boeing 707-323C, G-AYZZ, leased from American Airlines. The aircraft arrived at Gatwick on 11 June 1971 and the first service was flown that month. G-AYZZ was returned to the USA later that year, and for the 1972 season BCal had wanted to use a convertible passenger/freight 707. However, in the end the same aircraft returned for another lease from June 1972 to December 1973. Note the 'hybrid' colours that retained the American Airlines cheatline and unpainted roof in this shot at LGW on 10 August 1972. (Jacques Guillem collection)

◄ Cunard-owned British Cargo Airlines (BCA) flew six all-freight Douglas DC-8 Series 50s from their base at Gatwick after the airline was founded in August 1979. Formed by the merger of the unprofitable TMAC (Trans Meridian Air Cargo – which had DC-8s and CL-44s at Stansted) and the profitable IAS (International Aviation Services – which had two 707s at Gatwick), BCA was soon struggling with money problems. In order to slim down, in November 1979 it moved all operations to Gatwick, except the CL-44 and Shorts Belfast engineering functions. Sadly, the 'slimming' wasn't enough to survive high jet fuel prices and a massive reduction in customers needing specialist air freight services after the UK suffered a deep recession, and the receivers were called in March 1980. Seen landing at Gatwick in October 1979 is ex-IAS DC-8-54F G-BDHA, which ended its days in the USA after service with Arrow Air in 2001. (Richard Hunt collection)

▼ Originally delivered to BUA as G-ASIW at Gatwick in September 1964, this VC10 changed its colours in turn to Caledonian//BUA and British Caledonian, where it was named 'Loch Lomond'. From January 1974 BCal VC10s were leased to Air Malawi for a weekly Gatwick to Blantyre service before a deal was struck and G-ASIW was purchased outright by the Malawi government in late 1974. Four crews were trained by BCal on the BOAC simulators at Heathrow, while flight training was carried out at Prestwick. Painted in its new red and white colours, it was rolled out of the hangar at Gatwick on 22 November 1974 and made its first service to Malawi via a tech stop at Nairobi on 3 December with seats for eight first class and 111 tourist passengers. From early 1977 the flight went via Amsterdam and the airliner was kept busy, amassing sixty flight hours a week. The operational costs of keeping a single well-used VC10 in service caused the airline to cease flying it in October 1979 and it was positioned from Gatwick to Bournemouth in anticipation of a sale to the RAF. Three weeks' work in April 1981 made it airworthy again and it flew back to Malawi, where it was eventually scrapped in 1994. (Jacques Guillem collection)

◄ Tupolev Tu-134A CCCP-65035 is seen at Gatwick in October 1979 displaying special titles to show that Aeroflot had been given official airline status for the Moscow Olympic Games in the summer of 1980. These were the games that were boycotted by the USA and sixty-four other countries in protest at the Soviet invasion of Afghanistan, although UK athletes did attend. The Tu-134A was 2.1m longer than the original Tu-134, and it had more powerful engines and an APU positioned in the tail cone, it could seat up to eighty-four in a single class or twelve first class and fifty-four economy in a two-class arrangement, although Aeroflot said it carried sixty-eight. Aeroflot last operated a Tu-134 on mainline services in December 2007, and in May 2019 the Russian airline Alrosa made the last ever commercial Tu-134 flight. (Author)

▼ Having used its No. 2 engine (the only one with reverse thrust) to manoeuvre backwards into this position outside BCal's Hangar 1, this Aeroflot-liveried Yakovlev Yak-40 CCCP-87490 (which served as the Yak-40K prototype) was a very rare type at Gatwick when it visited in September 1976. Arriving via Copenhagen, it was on an Aviaexport sales tour and flew to Gatwick to allow BCal to assess the type as a replacement for the piston-powered de Havilland Herons that were operated by the BCal associated company, Sierra Leone Airways. BCal also had a management contract with Air Liberia and the aircraft was flown to Liberia to demonstrate its rough-field capabilities. British Island Airways also took a look at it as a potential Southampton–Channel Islands aircraft. The Yak returned to Ramenskoye (now called Zhukovsky), where it was operated by the Ministry of Aircraft Industry, and is currently preserved at Monino. Note the classic Ford Granada that brought out the BCal staff to have a nose around what was arguably the world's first 'regional jet' and the polar bear logo that apparently was collected in Canada. (Paul Robinson)

◀ Aeroamerica began commercial passenger flying from its base in Seattle in 1974 using six second-hand Boeing 720s with a single-class 149-seat arrangement on behalf of US travel clubs as well as a successful schedule from 1978 between Seattle and Spokane. The airline also flew passenger charters to Ireland, the Canary Islands and Turkey from a base in Berlin (Tegel) using 720s and 707s. Cargo charters were also flown from Berlin to Africa and the Middle East. Passengers were served by air hostesses in hot pants! Financial and safety concerns in late 1979 forced the airline to shut down. Leased to Aeroamerica from June 1978, Boeing 707-123B N7521A first arrived at Gatwick on a sub-charter for Laker that August and is seen here on 6 September having arrived empty from Berlin to carry out another sub-charter to Brussels. It was repossessed by Tiger Air in January 1980. (Christian Volpati collection)

➤ Lovely shot of Caledonian/BUA's Vickers VC10 G-ASIW 'Loch Lomond' taxying outbound at Gatwick on 4 September 1971. Like all VC10s, G-ASIW was built at Brooklands/Weybridge, the current site of the impressive Brooklands Museum where there is a complete VC10 plus the fuselage of another and an engineering mock-up on display. It made its first flight from Brooklands to Wisley on 30 July 1964 in the original BUA colours with the black cheat line and Union Jack on the tail. In 1970 it received this new colour scheme along with the short-lived titles Caledonian// BUA. In November 1974, G-ASIW was sold to Air Malawi as 7Q-YKH, and it continued to grace the ramp at Gatwick for another five years. (Peter Marson)

▼ Five Tupolev Tu-134s were bought by Polskie Linie Lotnicze (LOT) to replace Antonov An-24s on its European schedules and in some cases taking over routes flown by Ilyushin Il-18s. The first one arrived on 6 November 1968 and the airline later ordered seven of the upgraded and longer Tu-134A version. In 1974 LOT opened a charter flight department and this was responsible for charters for the next thirty years. This is Tu-134A SP-LHE in August 1979; it had been bought new in 1976 and was eventually withdrawn from use in 1993 and first moved to a museum at Lodz. In 2018 it was sold to another museum in Zruč in the Czech Republic. LOT opened a schedule to Gatwick in 2000, and in February 2005, LOT's charter subsidiary, Centralwings, flew its first service when a Boeing 737 flew from Warsaw to London Gatwick. (Author's collection)

◄ A murky evening in January 1977 saw Swedish airline Linjeflyg's Fokker F28 Fellowship SE-DGC awaiting its next load of passengers. Linjeflyg had been formed in 1957 to fly domestic schedules from its base at Stockholm using DC-3 Dakotas and from 1960 a large fleet of piston-engined Convair 440 Convairliners. From 11 May 1973 it flew Fokker F28 Fellowships, which were also used for medium-range IT charters in Europe. The airline eventually flew more than twenty F28s and replaced them with Boeing 737-500s. Linjeflyg was absorbed into SAS in 1993. Note the drop-down freight doors and the Bristol Britannia behind. (John Crawford)

▲ The Spanish national airline Iberia had been a regular visitor to Gatwick with piston-powered types such as the DC-4, Convairliner and Super Constellation. However, these were either Iberia aircraft operating on behalf of Aviaco or they were Heathrow diversions. After Iberia bought some new Caravelles in 1962, it flew them on domestic and European scheduled routes including services to Heathrow, but in a similar manner they also appeared at Gatwick from the summer of 1965 on Aviaco flights or diversions. This is 1962-vintage eighty-seater Caravelle VI-R EC-ARJ parked up in September 1971. All Iberia Caravelles were named after Spanish classical composers, this one is 'R Chapi'. Iberia initially flew thirteen Caravelle VI-Rs (Roman VI was used instead of '6') followed by an additional seven series 10Rs in 1967. It also leased a pair of Series 11Rs from Transeuropa in 1969 for freighting. All surviving Iberia Caravelles were passed to Aviaco from 1972, with the last IBE S210 flight occurring in March 1974. (Peter Bish)

◄ IAS (International Aviation Services) was a Gatwick-based all-freight airline that first started with a Bristol Britannia turboprop on wet-lease cargo charters to Africa on behalf of African International Airways. The fleet grew with more Britannias and a Canadair CL-44D until 1975, when it bought a pair of 40-tonne payload DC-8s from the USA for $4 million. The first to arrive was DC-8-54F N8782R, which is seen here landing at Gatwick the following month. As IAS was the first company in the UK to buy DC-8s, it took some time to obtain certification. The next year it was registered in the UK as G-BDHA, while the other DC-8 acquired the special registration G-BDDE 'Great Britain Douglas DC Eight'. IAS flew four DC-8Fs but also leased seven different Boeing 707s before it merged with Transmeridian Air Cargo in August 1979, creating British Cargo Airlines. Note the rudder trim tab appears to have the previous operator, Seaboard World's, colours. (Clive Grant)

► East African Airways ordered a pair of new Comet 4s in 1958 for routes from Nairobi to the UK (Heathrow), Karachi and Bombay as well as South Africa. The first service from Heathrow was in September 1960 and after the arrival of a third Comet in 1962, EAA sold off its last Canadair North Stars. EAA leased additional Comets from both BOAC and Dan-Air; 5Y-ALF (ex G-APDE) had been on lease from Dan-Air from February 1970 and is seen here after returning to Gatwick on 30 December 1970. EAA eventually stopped Comet flying in 1971. Such was the demand at Dan-Air for new cockpit crews that 'ALF' was re-registered as G-APDE and given Dan-Air London Training Unit titles while retaining the EAA colour scheme. It was based at Teesside, where it was used solely for crew training flights, although it did get flown to Lasham later and repainted in full Dan-Air colours. It remained a trainer until it was retired on 2 April 1973 and was later scrapped at Lasham. (Bob Wall)

➤ Lovely afternoon shot of Dan-Air's Boeing 707-321 G-AYSL. It was bought from Pan Am in January 1971 to start affinity group transatlantic charter services from Gatwick on behalf of CPS Jetsave that April. It was delivered to Newcastle by a Pan Am crew and commenced a series of crew training flights, after which it went to Stansted for some ARB modifications by ATEL. It made its first service for Dan-Air on 8 April 1971 from Gatwick to Niagara Falls in Canada. Over the next eight years it was leased to a variety of airlines, including BCal and British Airways, and in October 1979 it flew the airline's last 707 service. One of the 707s leased by Dan-Air in 1976 (G-BEBP) was destroyed in a crash in Zambia in 1977 while flying for Zambia Airways. (Martin Fenner collection)

◀ Check out the selection of classic jetliners in the background of this shot of Phoenix Airways' Boeing 707 at Gatwick on 6 August 1972. There are five Comets, Air Spain DC-8, Capitol DC-8, TIA DC-8, World DC-8, BCal B707 and another DC-8 in partial Universal colours. Formed in 1970 by a group of Swiss and German companies, it received its operator's certificate on 17 April 1971 enabling it to commence IT services from home base Basel with its new BAC 1-11-529FR HB-ITL. The company bought a Boeing 707 (HB-IEG) from Israeli Aircraft Industries (IAI) for long-haul services but its delivery was delayed while IAI converted it to a combi freighter, so Phoenix leased this 1959-vintage Boeing 707-131 N732TW from IAI for seven months in 1972. Both the 1-11 and 707 flew charters into Gatwick from Geneva. The airline did manage some 707 flying for Israeli airline El Al but bills went unpaid, Phoenix's operating certificate was withdrawn in March 1974. (Tony Merton Jones)

◄ Initially formed in 1976 by pilots Mike Davis (ex-Laker) and Terry Oldham (ex-British Airtours) with support from freight forwarders Hill and Delamain, Pelican Air Transport was based in Manchester with a pair of ex-Pan Am Boeing 707-321C freighters leased from ATASCO, although they (G-BEVN and G-BPAT 'Manchester Lass') were seen regularly at Gatwick. Pelican's first service from Manchester was with G-BPAT on 6 July 1978 with machine parts to N'dola, returning with grapes from Cyprus. Pelican also leased 707 G-BGIS from Scimitar for a period in 1980. Pelican ceased flying in July 1981 but by 1988 the Pelican Cargo name had reappeared as an independent air freight company based in Crawley and it is still in the freight forwarding business in 2020. Readers may recall that Air France Cargo also used the pelican logo on their freighters in the 1960s and '70s. (Jacques Guillem collection)

➤ After the fatal accident to Dan-Air's Boeing 707 freighter G-BEBP in May 1977, Dan-Air immediately sent an inspector to New York to check over a selection of old Pan Am 707-321Cs to find a replacement. This 1967-built 707-321C, N449PA, was chosen for a one-year lease from ATASCO, and because the airline's maintenance base at Lasham was so busy, it was flown to Tel Aviv on 10 June for IAI to convert it to UK specifications as G-BEVN. It returned to the UK on 7 July and was promptly sub-leased to IAS Cargo Airlines. Here it is on 17 July 1978 not long after the additional IAS titles were removed, leaving only 'Dan-Air – Operated on behalf of' on the fuselage. It was sub-leased to Tradewinds for a couple of months that summer before it made its last flight for Dan-Air on 28 September and returned to the lessor. (Chris Knott collection)

➤ An over-confident airline from Kuala Lumpur was Malaysian Southern Cross Airways. It pre-sold all the seats for its first three months of planned flights and then took that money to Pan Am and leased a Boeing 707-321 along with pilots and flight engineers in early 1971. The money mostly came from Australians and British ex-pats who wanted to fly to London on the cheap. The airline was forced by the Malaysian government to change its name to Southern Cross Airways (Malaysia) and the 707 9M-AQD was delivered via Gatwick on 10 June 1971. It subsequently flew its first service to London, taking eighteen hours with intermediate stops. Between June and September, a variety of charters were flown to destinations including Nairobi, Plaisance, Zaventem, Gatwick, Subang, Karachi, Essanboga, Luxemburg, Bangkok and Athens, but the airline neglected to pay for the fuel supplied by Esso Standard, which took the airline to court for the $700,000 owed. The airline had planned to acquire a second 707 but this never happened and the whole mess collapsed after Pan Am repossessed the 707 and parked it at Heathrow. (Peter Marson)

◄ According to surviving Gatwick log books, Swissair's Convair 990 Coronados started to appear at Gatwick late in 1963 when the illustrated HB-ICE 'Vaud' dropped in. Sister ship HB-ICB didn't make its first visit until New Year's Day ten years later in 1973. Swissair initially ordered seven Convair 990s, which were supposed to be more economic and faster than its direct competitors, the DC-8 and Boeing 707. However, the performance promises made by Convair were not fulfilled. When they were new, Swissair flew them to South America, West Africa and the Middle and Far East but late in their careers they were confined to European routes. After the 9/11 attacks, Swissair dramatically lost value and most flying had stopped by October 2001. The Swiss government threw money at the troubled airline, just keeping it alive until March 2002, when bankruptcy occurred. (Adrian Balch)

▲ Often seen in Europe in World Airways livery, Boeing 727-173C N693WA was leased to a variety of airlines around the world including United, Japan Air Lines, TOA Domestic and Pacific Southwest before this lease to Yemen Airways between 1977 and 1979. World Airways flew charters on behalf of the US military and its Boeing 707s, DC-8s, and 727s were often to be seen in Europe, including Gatwick, on this work. World's 727s sometimes operated flights within Europe. Yemen Airways began a period of expansion during the second half of the 1970s, leasing various aircraft including World 727s N690WA, N692WA, N693WA and N696WA. In 1994, the airline became Yemenia and it operated services to Gatwick, using Boeing 727-200s and later the Airbus A310. N693WA was bought new by World in 1967 and remained on its books until 1979. It was scrapped at Luanda (Angola) in the early 2000s. This aircraft was also a movie star: in the 1976 hijack film *Mayday at 40,000 Feet* it appeared in fictitious Transcon Airways livery alongside stars David Janssen and Ray Milland. (Author's collection)

◄ Parked on the '140s' awaiting its next load of holidaymakers in 1973 is 1960-vintage Boeing 707-436 G-APFG from BEA Airtours. The company received its first ex-BOAC 707 in February 1972. G-APFG was leased to BEA Airtours by BOAC from March 1973 and stayed after the airline became British Airtours the following year. Note the distinctive Rolls-Royce Conway engines with the fluted tail pipes. The 707 offered a greater payload as well as range advantage at a time when unprecedented increases in oil prices threatened the economics of overseas charter holidays. With a fleet of nine 707s from 1975, British Airtours operated IT charters to all six continents and occasionally provided a back-up for the parent company. The fuselage of G-APFG ended its days testing water-mist fire suppression equipment at Cardington. (Tony Eastwood collection)

◄ Not the best of shots but if you could see how filthy and colourless the original slide was, then you would be impressed with my Photoshop skills! Caravelle 10R JY-ACS 'Amman' is seen here taxying out to the western holding point in July 1970 for one of its twice-weekly services for flight RJ111 to Amman via Rome. Alia bought two new eighty-nine-seater Caravelles (JY-ACS and ACT) in 1965/66 and, carrying 'Alia The Royal Jordanian Airlines' titles in English and Arabic, they flew schedules to the European capitals of London, Frankfurt, Paris, Rome and Athens as well as shorter trips to Tehran and Kuwait. The first visit of an Alia Caravelle to the UK was when JY-ACT landed at LGW with the King of Jordan on 19 July 1966. An additional Caravelle was purchased in 1968 before all three were sold off in the early 1970s and replaced by Boeing 707s. (Author's collection)

➤ Initially founded by former BCal Managing Director M.A. Guinane in 1975, Scimitar Airlines came into being in 1978 after the British CAA granted it a cargo charter license, despite opposition from British Caledonian, Transmeridian and Tradewinds. It bought a pair of Boeing 707-321C freighters, G-BFZF and G-BGIS, and commenced charters to the Gulf area and to West and Central Africa with G-BFZF in late 1978. Based at Gatwick with its head office in Lowfield Heath, Scimitar wet-leased the two aircraft to IAS Cargo from the summer of 1979, but was shut down by the CAA in 1980 after the discovery that it was owned by Saudi nationals rather than a majority of British investors, as the law demanded at that time. Both 707s were later sold to Gatwick-based Tradewinds. (Author)

◄ Founded by the huge tour company Tjærborg in early 1962, Sterling Airways A/S initially appeared at Gatwick in September 1962 with its immaculate Douglas DC-6s. Its SE210 Caravelles, Series 12 OY-SAD seen here, first arrived in 1965 and became a regular sight at Gatwick until the last of them was retired in 1992. Sterling flew a total of thirty-four different Caravelles, second in number only to Air France. In December 1970 Sterling set a stage-length record for the Caravelle when it commenced a series of 'transatlantic' charters by flying ninety-nine passengers from Oslo to Gander, a distance of 2,268nm (4,200km), in five-and-a-half hours. Sterling's route map of 1972 shows that it served Chicago, Toronto, Hartford and Søndre Strømfjord, all via Keflavik where passengers had a meal while the aircraft was refuelled. (Author's collection)

➤ Buenos Aires-based freight hauler Transportes Aereos Rioplatense (TAR) commenced operations in 1971 with a small fleet of Canadair CL-44D freighters. Ex-Dan-Air and IAS Boeing 707-321C LV-MSG 'Gloria' is seen here at Gatwick on 7 July 1978, having flown in from Lasham in full TAR colours on 29 June with the British registration G-BEAF taped over the Argentinian one. It flew a test flight on the 7th, after which the tape was removed, allowing LV-MSG to become the airline's first jetliner. It departed on the 10th and entered service the next day. TAR leased a second 707 freighter in 1979 and used the aircraft for services to the USA and Europe. TAR shut down in November 1988. (Bernard King)

➤ Unsurprisingly never a common type to be seen at Gatwick, the VFW/Fokker 614 (only nineteen built) was remarkable for its unusual engine positioning. Air Alsace was formed as an air taxi operator in Colmar, France, in 1962 with small aircraft; in 1974 it commenced scheduled services to Lyon using Corvettes. As the company expanded, international services followed including Gatwick using F28 Fellowships. The company leased three 614s from 1976/77 and these mostly flew from Colmar to Paris. From 1981, the airline was merged with TAT-Touraine Air Transport. F-GATH, seen in May 1978, returned to the manufacturer in 1980 and was broken up for spares. (Richard Hunt collection)

◀ Initially calling itself Transpommair from March 1970, this Belgian charter airline, owned by Charles Pommé, was forced to change its name to Pomair Ostend in May 1971 after the first name was found to be used by another company. Its first airliner was SABENA's old DC-6B OO-CTK. After landing rights at fifty-five cities in the USA were acquired, an ex-Pan Am DC-8 was bought and registered OO-TCP (Transport Charles Pommé). This commenced worldwide long-haul operations in May 1971, and in May 1973, two DC-8-32s (OO-CMB and this one, OO-AMI) joined the fleet. It may be that the reason for its visit on 20 July 1974 was to operate a sub-charter for British Caledonian. OO-TCP flew in at least three different Pomair colour schemes, some of them featuring a winged mermaid on the fin. The colour scheme on OO-AMI came from its former owner, Belgian International Air Services. (Peter Marson)

▲ A fondly remembered jetliner from Gatwick's distant past was Wardair Canada's Boeing 727-11 CF-FUN 'Cy Becker', which first appeared at Gatwick on 2 May 1966, just a week after it was newly handed over at the now closed downtown Edmonton Municipal Airport. CF-FUN was the fourth 727 to visit Gatwick but the first to appear on a regular service; the other three were Lufthansa diversions from LHR that January. It was often claimed by Wardair that its 727 could fly direct from Canada to the UK, but on the occasions that it did it was via a tech stop in Frobisher Bay or Gander, certainly 'in Canada', but not a place they would have picked up many passengers! Wardair was, however, the first operator of the 727 on Atlantic routes. CF-FUN was Wardair's first jet and the first Boeing jet to be sold in Canada. (Richard Vandervord)

3

THE EIGHTIES

In 1983, the 'Satellite' pier was opened to mostly handle wide-bodied jets. Replacing the old North Pier, it was connected to the terminal by a driverless shuttle train called a 'Rapid Transit System' from which good views over the airport could be enjoyed. At the same time, the continued growth at Gatwick demanded an additional terminal to be built. The £200 million North Terminal (opened by the Queen in 1988) was built where a second runway had been proposed back in the 1970s. Traffic grew so much in the 1980s that, by 1987, the airport had overtaken New York JFK to become the world's second busiest airport for international passengers, with a total of 15.86 million. Gatwick in the 1980s will be remembered by many readers for its huge variety of airlines, but at that time it was an unfriendly place for spectators. The airport did much later build the always-busy Skyview that had shops and a viewing terrace complete with a Herald airliner and the nose of a famous Gatwick jetliner, a DH Comet. Skyview sadly closed in 2003 and now the only views of the ramp are from the perimeter fence or airside in the terminals.

◄ After the collapse of the Laker Airways empire in 1982, two of its fleet of three Airbus A300B4-203s (G-BIMA and G-BIMB) were bought by leasing company GPA Group Ltd, which leased them to Air Jamaica. Both were painted in the stunning Air Jamaica colours at Gatwick late in 1982 and were delivered the following month. Air Jamaica flew them until 1996, when they were returned to GPA and moved on to new operators. Interestingly, G-BIMA reappeared at Gatwick as TC-GTB with GTI Airlines (Turkey) in 1997 and G-BIMB visited with Irish airline TransAer in the summer of 1998. Note the tail logo is a doctor bird, the national bird of Jamaica. (Mike Axe)

▲ British Island Airways leased this single BAC 1-1-432FD G-AXMU to Gatwick-based Virgin Atlantic Airways to allow it to provide a feeder service from Europe (Maastricht in Holland) to Gatwick so passengers could connect to Virgin's transatlantic long-haul schedules. The lease lasted from January to April 1985, after which the aircraft was ferried to Lasham where it was prepared for a lease to Air UK. BIA had previously leased it to Air Ecosse and Airways International Cymru. The aircraft later became one of many 1-11s that flew for Okada Air (some were ex-British Caledonian) in Nigeria. BIA also leased 1-11s to Air Florida for connecting services to Amsterdam. (Author)

▲ Easily one of the smartest colour schemes to be seen at Gatwick in the 1980s belonged to Korean Air. In 1986 the airline flew as far as Zurich with DC-10s and Boeing 747s and from September 1988 it extended the route from Seoul to London Gatwick via Anchorage with a Boeing 747. The weekly service to London was later increased to three times a week and daily from 2004, although Gatwick lost out as the airline switched to Heathrow in 1991. However, Korean did return briefly to Gatwick in April 2012 with a Boeing 777 service three times a week. This is HL7458, a 747-2B5B first flown in 1981 and delivered new to Korea. (Author)

77

▲ A hugely significant event in the history of the BAC 1-11 was the order for six Series 424s from Romanian national airline TAROM (Transporturile Aeriene Române or Romanian Air Transport) in 1968. It became the only East European airline to order the type and, perhaps more importantly, Romania went on to build the 1-11 under licence in its own factories. TAROM 1-11s first appeared at Gatwick on schedules and charters in 1968, and after the schedule switched to LHR in 1970, the 1-11s continued to be regular visitors on charters until the early 1990s. BAC 1-11s built in Romania were known as ROMBAC 1-11s, but despite high hopes of a long production run, in the end only nine were completed. YR-BCL seen here in the summer of 1980 is a ROMBAC 1-11 Series 525FT built in 1977. This was later one of two Romanian 1-11s leased by BIA using Romanian cockpit crew with BIA cabin crew in 1987. (Author)

◄ Delta Air Lines (DAL) was eager to begin service to London, so it leased two L-1011-100 TriStars from TWA and inaugurated the DL11 Atlanta–Gatwick route on 30 April 1978. The -100 model had extra fuel capacity and higher take-off weight needed for the transatlantic route; however, it had the lower-thrust RB211 engines, so it was limited in its capability. These two leased L-1011-100s were later converted to -200 standard with higher-thrust engines. Here is L-1011-250 TriStar N1739D at Gatwick in July 1986; only six of these uprated long-range versions were completed using late model L-1011-1 aircraft as a basis. They had 269 seats with twelve 'sleeper seats' in first, fifty-four in business and 203 in economy in the awful 2-5-2 layout. DAL was the world's largest operator of the TriStar with seventy of the total 250 examples flown between 1973 and 2001. It flew them to forty US cities and thirty-nine international destinations. (Author)

▲ A new entrant to the North Atlantic cheap fare game was People Express (PEX). Using leased ex-Braniff Boeing 747s, its first service from New York arrived at Gatwick on 26 May 1983 after its approval to operate had been expedited. This was after the US authorities threatened to remove bilateral licence agreements for British Airways and BCal unless PEX operations were approved quickly. With fares starting at $149 each way, flights were soon sold out. Interesting to note is that PEX was the first US carrier to charge for checked baggage and for food or drinks aboard. The service was a great success and by 1986 PEX was offering first-class transatlantic tickets, too. It expanded to a fleet of seventy-five aircraft but the enormous debt it carried caused PEX to file for bankruptcy protection in February 1984. However, the company survived to merge with Continental Airlines in 1987. (Mike Axe)

➤ A regular sight at Gatwick for several years from 1983 were the freighter 707s of Zarkani Aviation Services (ZAS). ZAS owned or leased eleven 707s, including 707-328C SU-DAA seen here in November 1984. Based at Cairo International Airport, ZAS was formed in 1982 by two brothers, Sherif and Amir Zarkani; they commenced operations on 23 November 1982 with a flight from Cairo to Gatwick via Amsterdam. Apart from their cargo schedules and charters, they also flew scheduled passenger services using MD-80s and Airbus A300s, both types making appearances at Gatwick. In 1994, the Egyptian Civil Aviation Authority revoked ZAS's permission to fly on many domestic and foreign routes, which were handed to the state-owned Egypt Air. ZAS the airline was declared bankrupt in 1995 but the Zarkani name still survives as a ground handling company. (Author)

▲ In May 1981, BCal sold seven BAC 1-11 Series 200s to Pacific Express for services on the West Coast of the USA. The first to depart Gatwick was G-ASJC on 10 December for the nine-hour fifty-minute trip to Bangor via Goose Bay. G-ASJI is seen here outside the BCal maintenance area on 25 January 1982, prior to its transatlantic delivery two days later. G-ASJE was the last to go on 10 June and its departure marked the end of sixteen years of fantastically reliable BAC 1-11 Series 200 service with BCal. G-ASJI (illustrated in original BUA colours elsewhere) remained in the USA for the rest of its life, flying for Cascade Airways, Florida Express and Braniff Airways before it was scrapped at Orlando in 1991. (Steve Fowler)

➤ Aero O/Y Finnair ordered its first batch of three Caravelle IAs in January 1958. These started to arrive in 1960 and were immediately put to use on Finnair's European schedules. They were converted to Series IIIs and after Finnair had decided that the 2,300km range Series 10B3 was just what it needed, the IIIs were traded in and eight new 10B3s were ordered. Series 10B3 OH-LSG, seen here on a charter flight on 9 June 1982, was delivered in June 1966 and carried on in service until it was sold to Altair (Italy) in 1984 as I-GISU. Finnair continued to be seen at Gatwick right through into the twenty-first century using, at various times, four DC-8s, twenty-six DC-9s and twenty-two MD-80s. (Author)

▼ A colourful visitor to Gatwick commencing on 4 May 1978 was one of the world's oldest airlines, Aerovias Nacionales de Colombia (Avianca). It leased its first Boeing 707 from Pan American way back in 1960 to replace Constellations on services to New York. After Avianca received its first Boeing 720Bs, the 707 was returned and the type didn't reappear in the fleet until 1976, but they then served right through until 1991. This is 707-321B HK-2015 at Gatwick in July 1987 on the weekly Thursday afternoon run from Bogota via Madrid, wearing the stunning red colours that the company adopted in 1970. The airline also occasionally used a pair of Boeing 747s on the Gatwick service. Its sister ship HK-2016 made sad headlines when it ran out of fuel on a flight to New York and crashed, killing seventy-three passengers and crew. The airline last served Gatwick in 2011 and currently flies direct to Heathrow. (Author)

◄ Caribbean Airways leased Douglas DC-8-63 8P-PLC from International Air Leases in October 1986 and this became a rare one to photograph at Gatwick as it only made a few visits prior to its return to the leasing company that December. It first visited on 1 November on a schedule that included Frankfurt, Brussels, LGW, Bridgetown and St Lucia. Its last appearance was on 15 December before it was replaced by a sub-leased Cargolux Boeing 747. Carrying the titles 'Caribbean Airways – The National Airline of Barbados', it brought back memories of Laker's outfit 'International Caribbean Airways' that was also given the same subtitle back in the early 1970s. 8P-PLC also carried a sticker announcing it was 'Operated by Overseas Airways'. Over the next couple of years, the airline appeared with three different Lionair 747s, some carrying additional Orionair or Airtours titles. (Author)

◄ Dan-Air was switched on when it came to finding airlines to which it could lease its spare aircraft during the quiet winter months. Boeing 727-46 G-BAEF was sent off to Colombia as HK-3384X to fly for ACES (Aerolíneas Centrales de Colombia) in November 1987 and is seen here looking somewhat battered on its return to Gatwick in January 1988. In 1984/85 it had previously been sent on lease to Royal Air Nepal as 9N-ABV. Dan-Air Boeing 727s were also leased to GAS Air Nigeria, LACSA Costa Rica, Avianca Colombia, Air Malta and Sun Country USA. Dan-Air also leased in examples from Ariana Afghan and SAN Colombia. Interestingly, G-BAEF ended her days back in the wilds of Colombia, where she was scrapped in 2005 after service with Aero Republica Colombia from 1995 as HK-3840X. (Author)

➤ Gatwick-based Anglo Cargo bought its first Boeing 707-338C, G-BDEA, from BCal in December 1983 for worldwide cargo charters and commenced flying in January 1984. G-BDEA was given the name 'The Capt. Keith Hooper', after Keith had passed away. He was intended to be Anglo's chief pilot, but he sadly died before the company started trading. In October 1989, Anglo leased 707-338C G-EOCO from HAECO and then immediately sent it off to San Antonio, Texas, to be fitted with a $3 million set of engine hush kits. Both these Gatwick 707s could carry 40 metric tons of freight and they were eventually converted to E-8Cs with the USAF. G-BDEA was still operational in the USA in 2019. Anglo had two other freighters, Boeing 757F G-OBOZ and BAC 1-11 G-TOMO, which was registered such because the airline was run by Terry Oldham and Maggie Oldham. Anglo shut down in January 1992. (Author)

➤ A murky lunchtime trip over to the BCal maintenance area in the CAA control van allowed the author to clamber up the side of the earth bank that provided a jet blast and noise break so as to record the delivery flight of BCal's brand new Airbus A310 'John Logie Baird – The Scottish Television Engineer' on 19 March 1984. It went straight to the maintenance area carrying French test registration F-WZEF with its British registration just visible above the A310 wording on the fuselage. Why it then flew back to Toulouse via Paris four hours later we don't know, but the following afternoon it reappeared marked as G-BKWT. A few hours later, sister ship G-BKWU arrived via the same route and after a beat-up of the runway it joined WT on the ramp. WT made its first scheduled service for BCal on the 25th to Douala and Lusaka, and brought home Prince Charles from an African tour while WU made a series of crew familiarisation flights. (Author)

◀ Douglas DC-9-15 I-TIGI, seen here blasting off from Gatwick on 7 April 1980, was bought from Hawaiian Airlines by Itavia in 1972. Initially called Società di Navigazione Aerea ITAVIA, it commenced domestic services in Italy in 1959 using de Havilland Herons and Doves. After a period of shutdown, Itavia upgraded to a fleet of HP Dart Heralds from 1963 (five operated in total) until jets in the shape of F28s and new DC-9-15s were acquired. Additionally, larger DC-9 types were leased from 1974 and seven of their airline's total fleet of eleven appeared at Gatwick starting in 1972. Two months after this shot was taken, I-TIGI exploded in mid-air and crashed into the sea off Naples in mysterious circumstances. The cause of the crash that killed all eighty-one aboard has never been found, but the main theories are a bomb or an errant missile. (Clive Grant)

◄ Photographed from the ATC tower on its second visit to Gatwick on 15 April 1987, Boeing 707-369C ST-AIX had previously arrived on the 13th for a freight charter to Lagos. Here it is inbound from Malta using call sign GS408; it departed on the 17th as Sudanair 1161 to Khartoum via Amsterdam. Sudan Airways is an airline with far greater associations to Heathrow than Gatwick; however, Gatwick's first ever foreign-scheduled airline service was a Sudan Airways Viscount to Khartoum in 1959. ST-AIX led a fairly stable life, beginning with Kuwait Airways, then moving to Sudan Airways, where she plied her trade as a freighter until some point in the middle 1990s when she was taken out of service at Khartoum and reduced to spare parts. (Author)

▲ Los Angeles-based Total Air was formed in 1984 and flew its first charter service on 4 October from Los Angeles to San Diego to collect passengers for onward service to Honolulu. Total was managed by Ron Hansen and it appears that it was connected to Total Tours of Hawaii. After World Airways withdrew from the Baltimore to Gatwick route, Total took it over and flew two of its three TriStars N701TT/N702TT/N703TT on a schedule to Gatwick until the airline changed its name to Air America in November 1986. The Air America timetable for December 1986 shows the airline flew twice a week into Gatwick, arriving at 0845 on Mondays and Thursdays from Baltimore/Washington, having started from Los Angeles. Air America, still with the same TriStars, collapsed in 1990. N703TT, here in March 1987, reappeared at LGW as C-GTSZ with Air Transat. (Author)

◄ United flew a total of eighty-eight different Boeing 747s made up initially of twenty-three -100s, the first of which arrived in 1970, followed by ten -200s, forty-four -400s and eleven (ex-Pan Am) 747SPs. After forty-seven years of service (the longest continual operation of 747s by any US passenger carrier) United made its last ever 747 schedule with a special 'Tribute' trip to Honolulu from San Francisco in November 2017. Prices for the one-way trip started at $550 and all the seats were sold in two hours. The trip commemorated United's very first 747 service on the same route on 23 July 1970. The air hostesses wore 1970s-style uniforms and passengers were served 1970s' inspired meals, while the in-flight entertainment was also from those times. N4727U, seen on 24 July 1983 on a summertime weekly charter from/ to JFK, was named 'Robert E Johnson' after the long-serving retired executive vice president of the airline. He wrote a book, *Airway One: A Narrative of United Airlines and Its Leaders*. (Author)

➤ Your author has always had a soft spot for any aircraft from Egypt so I was disappointed not to catch this rarity in Gatwick on 5 July 1988. It arrived with a full load of suntanned passengers from Palma on a sub-charter for Air Europa that morning as AEA168, and a couple of hours later a load of pale-skinned Brits were sped off to Palma on AEA169. North African Aviation (NAA) was a charter airline that commenced operations in 1985 using a Shorts 330 leased from Fairflight. It also operated a fleet of crop-spraying Cessna types from Embaba in Egypt. This Douglas DC-9-51 SU-BKK was bought new by Swissair in 1975. It was acquired by NAA in June 1988 and quickly leased to Oasis International the following month. It was returned to lessor GPA that December. (Mike Axe)

◄ Montana Flugbetrieb was a Vienna-based long-haul charter outfit that made both passenger and freight flights, starting in late 1976 with a trip to Bangkok after it had taken delivery of Boeing 707-138B OE-IRA on lease from Boeing. This 707-138B, OE-INA, was delivered in July 1977 and is seen here having some minor maintenance on its No. 3 engine on Stand 19 on 20 April 1981. It had arrived from Vienna as OF121 with twenty-eight passengers and returned to VIE the same day with 166 aboard. Charters were flown to Mexico, Mombasa, Ceylon and Thailand, and from May 1980 to New York. Both 707-138Bs were sub-leased to a variety of airlines including Air Ceylon, Aer Lingus, EL AL, JAT and Alitalia. A Boeing 707-396C (OE-IDA, ex-C-FZYP of Wardair) joined the fleet in December 1978 and was also sub-leased to other airlines. It was seized by US Customs at Houston, Texas, in May 1981 while smuggling arms to South Africa. Two months later, Montana was bankrupt and ceased all flying with both 138Bs parked up at Vienna. (Author's collection)

➤ Istanbul-based freight airline BHT (Boğaziçi Hava Taşımacılığı), which translates as Bosphorus Air Transport, made its first visit to Gatwick from Istanbul with TC-JCF full of freight in August 1988. Several visits were made over the next few months using flight numbers BHT6301/6302, all with freight inbound and empty outbound. TC-JCF 'Beylerbeyi' is seen here on 6 October 1988 taxying on to stand at Gatwick. A subsidiary of the Turkish national airline THY, BHT had two 707-321Cs, the other being TC-JCC 'Üsküdar' which, according to the records kept by the Gatwick Aviation Society, didn't visit. The airline was liquidated by the Turkish government in May 1989. (Author)

◄ Brand new Boeing 737-2T4 N54AF was acquired on lease from GATX by Air Florida in January 1980. In May the following year it was sub-leased to Gatwick-based Air Europe for the summer months before returning to Florida in October to start the busy winter period there. In 1982 the same sub-lease occurred but this time it was registered in the UK as G-BJXM. This deal was part of a lease-swap with Air Florida, whose seasonality was opposite to Air Europe's. Initially, Air Europe sent three 737s to Florida for the winter 1980/81 season and the US airline sent two 737s over to the UK for the following summer. This transatlantic deal collapsed in the spring of 1983 after Air Florida struggled to provide aircraft on time and was also losing money. (Author)

➤ According to the files of the Gatwick Aviation Society, twenty-seven different Aeroflot Ilyushin Il-86s visited Gatwick, starting in October 1982. They arrived from Leningrad (now St Petersburg) and Moscow SVO. Here is CCCP-86058 in October 1983 pushed back and nearly ready to taxi out. Note the figure of the ground handler by the nose wheel. He is about to unplug his headset from the aircraft before walking back towards the stand, where he will show the captain that he has removed the steering bypass pin, thus allowing the aircraft to steer itself again. The Il-86 was the Soviet's first effort at a wide-bodied airliner and, although only 106 were built, it was popular with passengers, especially as you could carry your own heavy luggage on to the aircraft and stow it in the lower deck. Il-86 operators to visit Gatwick in the 1990s were Armenian Airlines, Pulkovo and AJT Air. (Author)

▲ Featured in the previous *Classic Gatwick Propliners* book with one of its magnificent Douglas DC-6s, the Slovenian national airline Adria Airways had survived with various titles since it was first formed in Ljubljana in 1961. In 1969, Adria added its first ever jetliner to its fleet of four DC-6Bs when it bought a 115-seater McDonnell Douglas DC-9-30. As business grew, Adria also leased a variety of types including a Caravelle, a DC-8 and a BAC 1-11. This DC-9-32 YU-AJF was first operated by Pan Adria, which flew it on services to Gatwick in 1973/74. Service with Inex Adria, then Adria Airways, followed before it was leased to British Midland (BMA) in October 1986. It is seen here still in BMA colours in October 1988 just before it was leased for a second time to BMA. Adria was one of several airlines including Germania, FlyBmi, Thomas Cook Airlines, Wow, Jet Airways, XL Airways and Aigle Azur that failed to survive the onslaught of the low-cost carriers and collapsed in 2019. (Author)

◄ The Civil Aviation Administration of China (CAAC) first bought Boeing jetliners in 1972 with an order for ten 707s for use on international services to Japan, Europe and the USA. Several of these appeared at Gatwick on charters starting in 1974. CAAC started a scheduled once-a-week Sunday service CA937 PEK–KHI–FRA–LGW on 16 November 1980. Initially with an American-registered B747SP, it changed to a B707 in January due to very light loads. The 747SPs returned from March 1982. From 1984, CAAC became the regulatory body for civil aviation in China and Air China took responsibility for all international services. After an agreement in December 2017, the number of weekly flights between China and the UK was increased by 50 per cent. In 2020, before Covid-19 hit, we had the following flying to Gatwick – Air China, Cathay Pacific, China Eastern, China Southern and, from Taipei, China Airlines. (Author)

▲ Hong-Kong-based Cathay Pacific received its first Rolls-Royce-powered Boeing 747-267B in July 1979. The choice of engines was a smart move as they were compatible with their TriStar fleet (also regulars at LGW). The airline's big breakthrough came in 1980 when it secured traffic rights to serve London (Gatwick) and the first CX 747 arrived via Bahrain on 16 July 1980. Cathay upgraded its huge 747 fleet with -300s and later -400s, and its last 747 service was made from Hong Kong to Tokyo in October 2016. That year saw the airline return to Gatwick after nearly twenty-three years serving Heathrow as its London gateway. A four-times-a-week non-stop schedule to Hong Kong commenced that September with Airbus A350-900s. Two other carriers had flown this route, Oasis Hong Kong in 2006–08 and then Hong Kong Airlines in 2012. Series 367 VR-HIJ, here in October 1986, was sold to Pakistan International in 1999. (Author)

➤ Not many Soviet-built types have made it into this book but one type was a regular at Gatwick, the Tupolev Tu-134. Right through into the 1990s, Tu-134s have appeared in the colours of Aviogenex, Balkan, Aeroflot, LOT, Interflug, Air Ukraine and Greenair. This one was flown by Turkish company Nesu Air, which had been formed in 1983 as an air taxi operator but only commenced international charters in March 1988 with an Istanbul to Hamburg service. In addition to a pair of 134s, which were leased from Aviogenex, Nesu also flew a leased Boeing 727 and a Douglas DC-3 Dakota (for enthusiast flights), and they even bought five Hansa Jet business jets. High costs and financial problems after the Gulf War caused Nesu to fold in late 1989. Tupolev Tu-134A-3 YU-AJA is seen on 30 October 1988. (Mike Axe)

◀ Transporturile Aeriene Române (Romanian Air Transport or TAROM) Ilyushin Il-62 YR-IRC at Gatwick 31 July 1982 waiting for an outbound Boeing 737-200 to taxi behind it before pushing back from Stand 26 on the end of the centre finger. Note the all-moving tailplane is already set for take-off and the wheeled tail support is tucked away, leaving its wheels poking out to act as a tail skid in case of over-rotation on take-off. Built at Kazan in March 1975, YR-IRC survived nearly twenty years of service in Romania and was put up for sale in 1998. It ended its days as EX-62100 at Manas Airport in Kyrgyzstan after service with Quadrotour Aero. It is interesting to note that TAROM had shown interest in buying new VC10s but ended up with this Soviet-built lookalike instead. It bought three new Il-62s and later a pair of the uprated Il-62Ms. (Author)

▲ Formed in April 1985, Transwede Airways AB commenced IT charters to the Mediterranean for Royal Tours using a pair of 109-seater Sud Aviation Super Caravelles: SE-DEH, bought from Finnair, and LN-BSE (seen here at Gatwick in July 1985), which was leased from K/S Aircharter. LN-BSE became SE-DHA in 1986 after it was bought outright and the same year Transwede also leased Caravelle SE-DEC and bought SE-DEB. This fleet of four was reduced to three when SE-DEC crashed on take-off at Arlanda in January 1987. Transwede supplemented the Caravelles with a pair of MD-83s and as business grew so did the fleet with a Boeing 737-200, two Boeing 737-300s, two MD-87s, seven Fokker 100s and another pair of MD-83s. Transwede went on to fly Stockholm–Gatwick schedules in 1991 but after company restructuring the name disappeared at the end of 1997. (Author)

▲ Coming in over the threshold of Runway 08R in July 1982 is C-GXRC, a DC-10 Series 30 of Wardair Canada. Named 'W.R. Wop May' after the famed Canadian First World War flying ace who became the last Allied fighter pilot to be pursued by von Richthofen (the Red Baron) before he was shot down, this DC-10 served Wardair for ten years and was a regular at Gatwick after its delivery in November 1978. In 1988, Wardair was flying daily to Gatwick from Toronto using A310s and DC-10s on the WD100/101 schedule. This DC-10 later became a freighter and was last seen parked up in Miami in 2019. (Richard Vandervord)

◄ Martinair Holland's Douglas DC-10-30CF PH-MBP operated a once-a-week service for Air Seychelles from November 1984 until October 1985. The usual operation was to position in from Amsterdam on a Friday afternoon, then depart to the Seychelles via Frankfurt on flight HM701. It returned SEY–FRA–LGW as HM702 arriving Saturday evening, then repositioned to AMS as HM702P. Prior to this lease, the service was operated from 1983 by BCal with a leased DC-10 and then from November 1985 they used Air France Airbus A300 F-BVGM in the simple but stunning Air Seychelles colours. This aircraft was also leased to Garuda and Philippine Airlines before ending up with the Royal Netherlands Air Force as a KDC-10 tanker. At the end of 2021 it will be sold to Omega Air Inc. (Author)

▲ The success of the Laker Airways Skytrain enterprise, which eventually took off for New York from Gatwick in September 1977 with passengers paying £59 for a one-way ticket, encouraged Laker to try something similar in Europe. On 10 April 1979 Laker ordered ten Airbus A300s (G-BIMA to G-BIMJ) and began campaigning for up to 630 low-fare routes in Europe. The CAA refused to license these operations and Laker planned to take the CAA and Department for Trade Industry (DTI) to court. Laker's first A300B4-203 was delivered in January 1981 and entered service on the 'Metro' route from Manchester to Zurich. Only two more A300s joined the fleet before the airline collapsed in February 1982 with debts of £270 million. Laker bounced back by starting Laker Airways (Bahamas) Ltd in 1992, operating Boeing 727s from Fort Lauderdale, and later Laker Airways Inc., which flew DC-10s on charters to Florida from the UK, including Gatwick. (Author)

▲ Captured arriving at Gatwick from Hanover on 29 April 1986, the first of Dan-Air's only wide-bodied airliners was leased from Hapag Lloyd until December that year. It arrived as DA99T D-AHLJ and was quickly re-registered as G-BMNA, although it remained in this hybrid colour scheme. It made its first service to Alicante on 3 May. Dan-Air's second A300, G-BMNB, also came from Hapag Lloyd but was bought outright in December 1986 and fully painted in Dan-Air colours. The third and final A300, G-BMNC, was leased from Guinness Peat Aviation in the summer of 1988 and made Dan's last A300 service in October 1990. G-BMNA was fitted with 312 passenger seats in a popular 2-4-2 layout; each Airbus had a crew of three, plus nine cabin staff. G-BMNB had seating for 336 and reportedly had long-range tanks, which made it ideal for services to Israel and the Canaries. Note the hyphen between the Dan and Air is now a little aeroplane silhouette. (Author)

➤ Tracing its origins back to TABSO, which was originally a joint Soviet/Bulgarian airline that flew to Gatwick from 1963 with Ilyushin Il-18s, Balkan Bulgarian Airlines upgraded to Tupolev Tu-134 (from 1968) and Tu-154 jetliners (from 1972), allowing Balkan to expand its IT charter operations. After the country ditched communism, the Bulgarian authorities allowed new airlines such as Air Via and Hemus Air to take a slice of the market and Balkan lost its monopoly on scheduled and charter services. Bulgaria also fell out of favour with tourists from Western Europe and by the start of the twenty-first century the airline was suffering financial problems that a privatisation couldn't cure. It was bankrupt in 2002 and was succeeded by Bulgaria Air. This is Tu-154B-2 LZ-BTU in October 1986, one of thirty-five Balkan/Bulgarian Tu-154s of various marques that visited Gatwick. (Author)

◄ This well-travelled Boeing 707-327C, N707ME, appeared at Gatwick on transatlantic charters in the early 1980s. Originally delivered to Braniff in 1967, it survived three years on lease from International Air Leases to Arrow Air from 1981 while still retaining the blue and yellow cheat line from its service with Singapore Airlines. With the R/T call sign 'Big A', Arrow Air could trace its ancestry back to 1946 but it was in 1981 that this Miami-based outfit got into jet cargo charters with DC-8s, many of them used for US military contracts. In December 1981 it flew a Denver to Gatwick service on behalf of Western Airlines for three months, and in December 1982 it flew its first service from Tampa to London, but this route was cancelled in 1984. Arrow also flew to Gatwick with DC-10s in the mid 1980s but was more often seen using its stretched DC-8-62s, -63s and 73s. The company folded in 2010. (Author's collection)

One of the author's favourite spots to shoot slides on the ramp was when aircraft had pushed back from the south side of the centre finger. The grass island between taxiways 1 and 2 gave a bit of extra colour to the image and you were normally positioned with the sun behind you. However, you were sometimes parked in the middle of the taxiway at a pretty busy airport, so timing and a good lookout were of the essence! Here is Jugoslovenski Aerotransport (JAT) Boeing 727-2H9 YU-AKK on a regular tourist run back to its home country in July 1986, just after the aircraft had returned from lease to Air Afrique for three years. Obviously no time to get it in the paint shop ... (Author)

▲ While waiting for some Boeing 737-200s to be delivered, and with additional schedules to be operated in the summer of 1987, Air Malta leased American Trans Air Boeing 727-51 N287AT that April. Many rotations to Malta from Gatwick were made that summer, with the aircraft bearing these typical short-lease decals of that era. It was returned to 'Am Tran' in September but was back at Gatwick in 1989 when it was leased to Bristol-based Paramount Airways, again in full ATA colours but with Paramount stickers. The following summer it was back again, this time for a few weeks' lease to British Airways, which again dropped it into Gatwick. Originally built in 1965 for Northwest Orient Airlines, this well-travelled 727 also flew for National, Pan American and Flight International Airlines. It was eventually scrapped in Oklahoma in 1994. (Mike Axe)

◄ Lionair was formed by Luxembourg companies Luxair (the national airline of Luxembourg) and Cargolux (Luxembourg's all-freight airline) in 1988 with a pair of old Pan Am Boeing 747-100s, LX-FCV and LX-GCV, with 492 passenger seats crammed into the fuselage. When Lionair flew charters to Puerto Plata, Santo Domingo, Barbados and Antigua, for licensing reasons it added the titles 'Caribbean Airways – The National Airline of Barbados'. Similarly, when operating to Orlando, it used the name of the US airline Orionair, which apparently caused some confusion as some passengers thought they were flying with the British charter airline Orion Airways. (Author)

◄ Super colourful Douglas DC-8-63 N4935C 'Stanvaste' of Surinam Airways (SLM) is seen here at Gatwick, 2 May 1987. It has had a hush-kit conversion to conform to noise restrictions and carries 'Quiet DC-8' titles on the engines as well as stickers proclaiming 'On lease to Monarch'. It was leased by Monarch from 30 April when it arrived from Luton, and was returned on 9 May after taking 217 passengers to Corfu. Originally delivered to Iberia Airlines in 1968, it was bought by Surinam Airways in July 1985 and was the only DC-8 owned by the airline, although from 1975 it did lease four others. Surinam, the smallest country in South America, used to be a Dutch colony (Dutch Guiana) and retained its close ties and tourist flights from the Netherlands even after independence in 1975. Despite the airline's small size, somebody has written its story, *Flying on Trusted Wings: Fifty Years of Surinam Airways*. (Mike Axe)

The airline business in Sierra Leone was for a long time connected to Gatwick thanks initially to British United Airways acquiring a 70 per cent stake in Sierra Leone Airways (SLA) in 1961 and being tasked with the day-to-day operation of the airline. BUA was also involved with the maintenance of SLA's Twin Pioneers and DH Herons back at Gatwick, and from November 1961, BUA flew a weekly non-stop Britannia service to Freetown from Gatwick for SLA. A BUA VC10 complete with Sierra Leone titles replaced the Britannia from November 1964. In 1982, SLA became Sierra Leone Airlines and the management contract with BCal (which took it over from BUA) was switched to Alia in Jordan. Alia leased Boeings to SLA; this 720B, JY-ADT 'Spirit of Friendship', and a couple of 707-320Bs, JY-AEB and AEC, for long-range services to Gatwick. (Author)

➤ Displaying its non-standard colours at Gatwick on 17 September 1982 is BAC 1-11 Series 416EK G-SURE. This was originally with Autair as G-AVOE but after sale to Air Manchester in April 1982, it was given this special registration. Air Manchester was not doing well at the end of the 1982 summer season so it contracted British Air Ferries (BAF) to operate its remaining 1-11, which was G-SURE. BAF painted over the Air Manchester red cheat line and the underside in dark blue and flew it in these hybrid colours for a few weeks until Air Manchester shut down in November. BAF received its first 1-11 in March 1990 and went on to become a major operator of the type as well as setting up a maintenance facility for them (World Aviation Support) at Southend. From April 1993, the airline became British World Airlines, which appeared regularly at Gatwick until shutting down in 2001. (Mike Axe)

▲ Linee Aeree Mediterranea, known as Aermediterranea, commenced ops in July 1981 with eight DC-9-32s after it was formed as a joint venture between Alitalia and ATI to replace Itavia. They were a regular sight with charter flights to LGW for a few years before the airline was wound up after the major shareholder, Alitalia, decided it was uneconomical to run both Aermediterranea and ATI. Aermediterranea was shut down on 1 April 1985 and all its staff and aircraft were transferred to ATI. The colourful fleet, with a livery based on the Alitalia design, was based at Rome Fiumicino and I-ATIQ, seen in September 1982, was named 'Sila' after a mountain region in Calabria. (Author)

◄ Arriving empty from Aden airport on 16 June 1985, this rare Boeing 707-336C stayed overnight and collected 33,000kg of freight before returning home via Jeddah the following day. Luckily the author was on hand with his trusty Canon camera to record its visit. Registered in South Yemen (formally Aden) to the national airline Alyemda, 7O-ACO had been a previous visitor as early as 1971 when it was owned by BOAC. Alyemda merged with Yemenia in 1996 and currently operates schedules around the Middle East. Too late a date for inclusion in this book was another, even rarer, Alyemda aircraft in the shape of Tupolev Tu-154 7O-ACT in August 1991. (Author)

➤ The successful Luxembourg-based freight airline Cargolux started ops in 1970, initially flying Canadair CL-44D turboprops and then later Douglas DC-8s all over Europe, North America and the Middle and Far East. Cargolux leased four different Boeing 707s including this one, 707-331C LX-BJV, which arrived empty at Gatwick on 12 October 1981 from Tripoli and loaded freight to return to Luxembourg the next morning. It reappeared on the 23rd with inbound freight from Tripoli and departed empty to Luxembourg. LX-BJV was a 'non-convertible freighter' and after Cargolux acquired Boeing 747s, it was sold in 1981 and flew for many different freight outfits in Libya, Ghana and the USA. It ended up in Miami, where it was scrapped in 1995. (Christian Volpati collection)

➤ Originally intended to join the Air Canada fleet as C-FTOF in 1974, this Boeing 747-233B Combi hung around with Boeing until it was delivered to Canada in March 1975 as C-GAGA. Air National (Air National Aircraft Sales and Service Inc.) leased it from Air Canada in the spring of 1983 and it is seen here pushing back from Gatwick's Satellite Terminal that September, operating flight OV602 for Overseas National. It only lasted another month with Air National before it returned to Air Canada. Air National had a mailing address in Monterey, California, and initially flew an odd mix of a Corvette and two Hansa Jets on freight flights before upgrading with a small fleet of DC-9-10s and a 727. Once Air National was approved for passenger charters, it leased C-GAGA and from February 1984 it leased another 747, LX-SAL, which first appeared at Gatwick in May 1984 from Philadelphia. The company filed for bankruptcy in September 1984. (Author)

▲ Tradewinds started out with Canadair CL-44D propliners on worldwide freight charters in 1968. After the airline was bought by Lonhro in 1977, it leased Boeing 707 N5772T, which was given the full Tradewinds colour scheme with the iconic sail on the fin. Other 707s were leased for short periods and three -323Cs and this -321C, G-TRAD, were bought outright. The airline enjoyed playing with the UK registrations as, in addition to G-TRAD, they had G-WIND and G-SAIL. Altogether, thirteen different 707s flew for Tradewinds. Note the Corrie Hill titles and CHS logo; this was a company set up by Scottish MP John Corrie and Robert Hill, who launched Corrie Hill (Scotland) on a £500,000 investment from Guinness Mahon Venture Founders Fund. They wet-leased G-TRAD for a three-times weekly scheduled cargo service from Prestwick to Hartford and Boston beginning in June 1984. CHS ceased trading three months later with debts of £70,000. (Author)

Set up as Inter European Airways by two former Dan-Air executives (Errol Cossey and Martin O'Regan) in 1978, the company was renamed Air Europe (AE) and commenced IT operations in May 1979. Initially buying a couple of new Boeing 737-200s, the airline flew on behalf of tour operator Intersun. AE made a deal with Boeing and British Airways (BA) to buy a pair of new 228-seater Boeing 757-200s. First to arrive in March 1983 was G-BKRM and, while waiting for No. 2, BA leased this example, G-BIKF, to AE for the summer of 1983. AE eventually went on to operate sixteen of the type. Based at Gatwick, the airline branched into scheduled flights as well as setting up subsidiary airlines abroad such as Air Europe Italy and Air Europa in Spain. Sadly, in March 1991, its parent company, the International Leisure Group, sought bankruptcy protection and grounded the airline's fleet, stranding 25,000 people. (Author)

The Spanish charter airline Spantax S.A. was a major player in the holiday traffic at Gatwick going right back to the early 1960s, when it flew DC-4s and later DC-7s. From 1967 Spantax appeared at Gatwick with its famous smoky and fuel-thirsty Convair 990 Coronados, a sight many enthusiasts will recall. A fatal DC-10 accident at Malaga in 1982 caused several tour operators to abandon the airline but it bounced back by replacing the fleet with Boeing 737s and MD-83s. However, the airline still struggled with finances and was eventually shut down in March 1988, leaving 7,000 passengers stranded all over Europe. This 737-229 OO-SDD appeared on lease from SABENA in the summer of 1987 before being re-registered EC-EEG. (Author)

➤ British Island Airways (BIA) BAC 1-11 Series 416EK G-CBIA (also illustrated elsewhere) with 'Air Florida' stickers by the front door in August 1983. According to Peter Villa, the MD of BIA, this deal 'caused no end of trouble getting approval from the UK Department of Transport!' It was classified as a 'change of gauge' service and once it was grudgingly approved, all four BIA 1-11 Series 400s were given Air Florida stickers for flights to Düsseldorf, Hanover, Amsterdam and Brussels to connect with Air Florida's daily DC-10 to Miami from Gatwick. The 1-11s carried all-British crews but flew with Air Florida 'Palm' flight numbers between May 1983 and July 1984. (Author)

▲ Thanks to slot restraints at Heathrow, the Air Seychelles name first appeared at Gatwick in 1983 when it started a weekly scheduled service from Mahé via Frankfurt on 26 October in conjunction with BCal. BCal's DC-10 G-BEBM carried 'Air Seychelles' stickers for the service, which had eighteen seats in executive class and 278 in economy class. The airline then leased a Martinair DC-10, followed by an Air France A300. Ahead of receiving a Boeing 767 in October 1989, the airline leased a pair of hush-kitted Boeing 707-324Cs in this striking and modern colour scheme, which even today looks stunning. Both 707s (S7-2HM and S7-4HM) had begun their service life with Continental Airlines in 1968. After their spell with Air Seychelles, both were painted up in Golden Horn (Turkey) colours in 1990 but they were never delivered and moved on to Angola Air Charter, which withdrew the depicted aircraft from service in the late 1990s at Luanda and used it for spares. (Author)

▼ Now here's a nice beast at LGW: Westar International Airways Boeing 707Q N2215Y on a sub-charter for World Airways on 12 July 1986. Normally World flew from Baltimore or Los Angeles to Frankfurt via Gatwick. N2215Y arrived empty from Frankfurt as WO33 and collected a full load of 186 passengers for return to BWI/LAX. Note the 'Tropical' titles from its lease by Fort Lauderdale-based Tropical Airways, which wanted to operate scheduled passenger and cargo services between New York and Georgetown (Guyana). Here it is lining up on runway 08; note the four red lights partway along the side of the runway; these are PAPIs (Precision Approach Path Indicators) that assist landing aircraft to follow the correct glide path – two white and two red lights signal a correct glide path, below the glide path they would see three reds and one white. N2215Y was converted to a 'Quiet' 707Q in 1985 with Comtran-designed hush kits by Tracor at Santa Barbara. (Author)

◀ Boeing's model 720 was initially referred to as the 717 and was designed for short/medium-range services in the US domestic market. Officially launched in July 1957, the type was first ordered by United Airlines. Compared to the 707 series 100, the 720 was 2.36m (7ft 9in) shorter and flew faster thanks to lighter fuel loads, a lighter wing structure and engines, and a revised inboard wing profile. Luton-based Monarch Airlines flew a total of seven Boeing 720Bs between 1971 and 1983, the type being the company's first venture into the jetliner market. G-BCBB was first registered in 1974 when Invicta leased it from American Airlines; this old lady is currently preserved at the Israeli Air Force Museum at Hatzerim as 4X-BYG. (Author)

◄ GAS Air Cargo (General and Aviation Services) was one of many all-freight outfits in Nigeria in the 1980s, most of them operating with the venerable Boeing 707. Others to visit Gatwick included UAS Cargo, EAS Cargo, DAS Air (an associated company), Merchant Express, Foremost Aviation and Thames Air. Formed in 1983, it was initially known as RN Cargo but changed to GAS in early 1984. Boeing 707-338C 5N-ARQ is seen here in October 1985 trundling outbound on Taxiway 8 past the control tower. Sister ship 5N-AWO managed to crash land two years running in 1991/92 but both times it was repaired. 5N-AYJ wasn't so lucky and was written off in a fatal crash near Luxor in 1988. (Author)

▲ Services to London (Heathrow) by Philippine Airlines (PAL) started back in 1947 with Douglas DC-4s, making PAL the first airline in Southeast Asia to fly to Europe. In 1954, flights to Europe were suspended by the Philippine government, and they did not restart until five years later. PAL received its first Boeing 747 (N743PR seen here in October 1987) in 1979 and used them on schedules to Gatwick. Flights to Europe were again stopped in 1998 but restarted to Heathrow in 2013 after the airline was banned from EU airspace due to poor safety ratings in 2010. Most of PAL's 747s were registered in the USA because financiers and lessors felt more secure when the aircraft were subject to US law. (Author)

◄ Thankfully the weather is being kind to the Dan-Air Engineering team who are changing the number four engine on this UAS Cargo Boeing 707 in the cargo area at Gatwick in October 1985. United Air Service leased this Boeing 707-351C 5N-ASY in 1983 to operate charter flights from Nigeria to other points in Africa and to Europe. The badge on the forward fuselage appears to say 'In association with EAS (NIG) Ltd'. The airline was renamed EAS Cargo in 1987 and ceased cargo operations in January 1992, but carried on flying scheduled passenger services with Boeing 727s and a Beech 200. (Author)

▲ Nigerian airline Okada Air was based in Benin City and in 1983 it bought its first four ex-British Caledonian BAC 1-11s, commencing scheduled services to destinations such as Abuja, Kano, Lagos and Port Harcourt. Prior to delivery, these 1-11s were all painted up at Gatwick and further examples bought from Quebecair and Britt Airways were also prepared there. Okada eventually owned twenty-eight (only twenty-five in service) different 1-11s, with examples joining the fleet into the early 1990s. The Nigerian government grounded all 1-11 operations by banning them in 2002. G-BKAV, seen here in October 1983, was originally Laker's G-AVBX and was later leased to BCal. It was one of the first four sold to Okada in September 1983 and is seen with its UK registration for test flights prior to becoming 5N-AOP. Okada Air also appeared at Gatwick with a Boeing 707 and a DC-8. By 2005, seventeen retired Okada 1-11s were all rotting at Benin Airport. (Author)

◄ British Caledonian Charter was formed in 1982 as a joint venture between BCal and the Rank Organisation. To better separate this airline from the parent one, it later became BCA Charter until 1985, when as part of an aggressive £1 million marketing promotion, it was relaunched as Cal Air International. Sporting huge 2.5m-high titles and a stunning red and white livery, its two ex-Laker DC-10s, G-BJZD and G-BJZE, were joined in March 1985 by G-GCAL. Cal Air had ordered two Boeing 737-400s in 1987 but the order was never fulfilled as in 1988 Cal Air was sold to Rank and renamed Novair. In 1991, G-GCAL (the third DC-10 built) joined the Project Orbis eye hospital programme as N220AU. (Author)

➤ Having joined the Gatwick-based Dan-Air fleet in 1972, Boeing 727-46 G-BAFZ was leased and then bought by Dublin-based Club Air in 1988. Club Air had been started in 1987 by Club Travel, an Irish IT operator. Club Air entered a leasing agreement with Virgin Atlantic that led to a combination of holiday and scheduled operations in this thinly disguised Dan-Air livery. Club Air's three Boeing 727s operated holiday flights from Dublin, while in one of Virgin's many sideline enterprises, EI-BUP operated its Luton–Dublin service, competing with the emerging Ryanair. The airline failed to compete and shut down in October 1988. Never to find settled employment again, having led a busy and a wearing early life on shuttle services in Japan, this example was scrapped in Zaire (Congo) in 1992. (Author)

◄ BAC 1-11- 416EK G-CBIA was once operated by Air Siam, which features elsewhere in this book with its Boeing 707. It was bought second-hand by British Island Airways in May 1979 and when they merged with Air Anglia, Air Wales and Air Westward in January 1980 to form Air UK, G-CBIA 'Island Ensign' was the only Air UK 1-11 to be given this controversial all-over blue colour scheme. The aircraft became virtually invisible at night under the airport's yellow sodium lighting. Note that in this shot taken in September 1980 it has the original engines; by the following summer it had been 'hush-kitted'. The Air UK 1-11s did occasionally operate scheduled BIA and later Air UK services, but only on an ad hoc basis. When the BIA name was revived in 1982 for the IT operations of Air UK, G-CBIA was repainted in BIA colours and flew from Gatwick until sold in Nigeria in 1989. (Author)

➤ In the summer of 1982, American Airlines (AA) was awarded its first European route connecting Dallas-Fort Worth (DFW) and London Gatwick courtesy of Braniff International's bankruptcy. AA chose to operate the route initially with 747s on this AA50/AA51 service. Here is Gatwick Handling's TUG 72 pushing back Boeing 747-123 'LuxuryLiner' N9674 from the Satellite Terminal on 26 September 1982 prior to flying the schedule to Dallas. The 747 was replaced by DC-10-30s on the DFW–LGW route on 2 November. Delivered to AA in 1971 with sixty-six first class and 300 economy seats, N9674 was sold to Pan Am the following year and eventually, converted to a freighter, it flew with Polar Air Cargo as N859FT until it was retired in 2001. (Author)

◄ Just scraping in to the cut-off date for this book is Nationair's Douglas DC-8 Series 61 C-GMXL in October 1988. Nationair had initially leased it from French carrier Point Air (hence the odd colours) in October 1987 then bought it outright in February 1988, but it is not thought to have been repainted in the full Nationair colours. Based at Montreal, Canada, Nationair was founded in December 1984 with stretched DC-8s and later flew Boeing 757-200s and 747-100/200s, both of which appeared at Gatwick on transatlantic charters. At one time Nationair had a fleet of twenty-four airliners but after one of its DC-8s crashed in Jeddah due to poor maintenance, it struggled with finances and was declared bankrupt in 1993. (Author)

◄ An interesting arrival on 15 September 1982 was this very scruffy Boeing 737-200 registered in Yemen as 4W-ABZ. It had been leased by Yemen Airways to Guinness Peat Aviation, which sub-leased it to Nigeria Airways for about a year. It arrived from Algiers and departed to Lasham the following morning, where it was given some maintenance prior to returning Lasham–Gatwick–Algiers (and presumably Nigeria) on the 20th. The author had seen this aircraft before when it visited Luton in 1977 in full Yemen Airways colours. Yemen Airways became Yemenia in 1978 and commenced services to Gatwick with Boeing 727s in December 1980. (Author)

◄ Boeing 727-200 CS-TBX 'Faro' of TAP Air Portugal was delivered in March 1980 and is seen here pushing back from the centre finger at Gatwick in September 1984. It was sold in 1991 and went on to join the fleet of one of the later versions of Pan American from 1997. One of thirteen 727s operated by TAP, it ended its days at Portsmouth, New Hampshire, in 2006. The world's last passenger flight in a Boeing 727 took place in January 2019 when Iran Aseman Airlines flew EP-ASB from Zahedan to Tehran's Mehrabad International Airport, marking an end to the 727's almost fifty-five years in service as a passenger aircraft. (Author)

▼ This Boeing 727-264 could do with a coat of paint, but when you read just what this aircraft had been through you will forgive it its looks! It arrived at Gatwick in April 1986 on a lease to Dan-Air from Aeron Aviation Corp still carrying its previous lessor's colours. Sun Country had leased it since September 1985 and operated it on services out of Minneapolis. It was soon repainted in full Dan-Air colours and flown on services with a US cockpit crew until it was re-registered as G-BMLP on 10 July 1986. Its last flight with Dan-Air was from Manchester to Lasham on 2 November 1992, where it was prepared for sale in Canada. Note the rare long hump on the roof from its time with Mexicana, when it was fitted with JATO rockets and the ADF antenna had to be repositioned in the roof. Genteel Dan-Air staff gave it the name 'Lumpy Papa' but others called it the 'Limping Prick'. There was huge controversy with this aircraft during its Dan-Air service as it had suffered major damage and a fire during a wheels-up landing at Acapulco while with Mexicana in 1983 and had to be partially rebuilt by Boeing. The UK media got hold of the story and accused Dan-Air of flying a patched-up airliner in the newspapers and on a special *World in Action* documentary. (Mike Axe)

◀ Based in Kansas City, Missouri, Global International Airlines flew summer transatlantic passenger charters to Gatwick for a couple of years in the early 1980s using a fleet of leased and owned Boeing 707s including N886PA, seen here in August 1983 one month before it was repossessed by Pan Am. Global began worldwide charter cargo flights in August 1978 along with a few passenger charters to Honolulu, Las Vegas and the Caribbean using Boeing 707s. From 1981, passenger charters to Amsterdam, London, Frankfurt and Paris saw Global's fleet appearing at Gatwick. The airline suffered from airworthiness regulations, union issues and was even suspected of gun running! Global's Boeing 747-133 C-FTOA also visited Gatwick in the summer of 1983 before the airline sought Chapter 11 bankruptcy protection in October 1983 after losing more than $5 million in a year and having its aircraft impounded at European airports for non-payment of fees. (Author)

➤ Only around at Gatwick from May to August 1985, BCA Charter was so named because the previous iteration, British Caledonian Airways Charter, which carried 'British Caledonian Charter' titles along with the full BCal colours, was causing passenger confusion between it and the main scheduled airline. BCal's Charter division had been formed in 1982 after the demise of Laker Airways with a 50/50 partnership with the Rank Organisation, enabling it to fly a pair of ex-Laker DC-10-10s to the usual Mediterranean resorts, Africa, the Canaries and the USA. From the end of the summer season of 1985, the BCA Charter identity started to disappear as it was replaced by a striking new red/white scheme when the charter arm was rebranded in a £1 million marketing effort to appear as Cal Air International. (Author)

▲ The author probably shot this picture out of the CAA control van window while keeping the heater full on in January 1982. Pushed back from the cargo area with the ground man about to disconnect the tow bar from the nose gear, Boeing 707-338C G-BFLD displays this odd colour scheme that belonged to DETA (Direcção de Exploração de Transportes Aéreos) Mozambique Airlines, which had sub-leased the aircraft from BMA in January 1979. The red DETA livery had been applied at Lasham in May 1980. Note that it still retains all the cabin windows but they are blanked off by the protective walls inside this freight configuration – it had a full-sized forward freight door on the port side. After years of freighting in the USA and then Nigeria in the 1980s and '90s, it ended its days at Manston in Kent. (Author)

◄ Sadly missed by many aviation enthusiasts are the 'three-holer' TriStars and DC-10s that were such a dominant part of the wide-bodied scene at Gatwick for many years. BEA Airtours, a subsidiary of British European Airways, commenced charter services from Gatwick with seven DH Comet 4Bs in 1970. The airline became British Airtours in 1974 and leased TriStars from parent company British Airways from 1981. TriStar 1 G-BEAL had been delivered to British Airways in late 1976 and was switched to British Airtours at Gatwick for IT flights in the spring of 1983. It was converted to a TriStar 50 in 1985 and over the next fifteen years flew for Caledonian Airways, Air Operations of Europe, Atlanta Airways, International Airways and finally Classic Airways. (Author)

➤ Air Inter made its first flight in March 1958 and began regular services in 1960 using DC-3s linking major cities in France. A fleet of Air France Vickers Viscount 700s were acquired in 1961, allowing major expansion, and in 1964 Air Inter added Nord 262s. Apart from a few sporadic appearances by Viscounts, the airline only started to appear more often at Gatwick in 1971 once it had acquired Caravelles; however, one of its Dassault Mercures (F-BTTH) did drop in way back in 1978. Air Inter was actually the launch customer for the Mercure but it was a commercial disaster with only twelve built. This rare type only ever flew with Air Inter, which operated ten of the twelve, and all ten of them visited Gatwick in the late 1980s with a 162-seat, all-economy layout. This aircraft, F-BTTF, is now preserved at Bordeaux-Mérignac. (Author)

▼ Established in 1965, Spanish charter airline Trans Europa (Trans Europa Compañia de Aviación S.A.) commenced ad hoc charter operations from Palma de Majorca to Spanish seaside resorts that September using a Douglas DC-7B. Two more DC-7s joined in 1966/67, allowing the airline to commence international IT charters before it upgraded to jets in the shape of a pair of Caravelle 11Rs, EC-BRX and EC-BRY, in 1969. Caravelle 10R EC-DCN is seen rolling out on Runway 26 complete with a cloud of black smoke from its reversers in April 1980. Transeuropa's (note that the airline name is now a single word) Caravelle fleet of eight appeared at Gatwick on charters for Aviaco. After this aircraft was sold to Hispania in April 1983 it continued to appear at LGW. Iberia and Aviaco later bought 60 and 40 per cent of Transeuropa respectively but the airline shut down in 1982. Note the lump under the forward fuselage housing Doppler radar to assist with long over-water routes or routes over areas with poor navaids. (Clive Grant)

◄ On short finals to Runway 26 at Gatwick in August 1985 is BAC 1-11 208AL EI-ANF 'St Malachy' of Aer Lingus. Delivered new to the airline in 1965 with a seventy-four-seat economy-class layout, it spent a few months on lease to LANICA in 1966/67 before providing continuous service in Ireland until all the airline's 1-11s were sold in 1991 and replaced by the ubiquitous Boeing 737. Before Covid-19, Aer Lingus was flying up to six times a day from Gatwick to Dublin using A320s with the occasional A321, but the airline also appeared at LGW with BAe 146s. A regular at Gatwick, EI-ANF ended her days, like many others, derelict in Nigeria after flying with Hold Trade Air. It was reportedly scrapped at Kaduna. (Author)

◄ This Boeing 707-399C previously graced the ramp at Gatwick after it had been delivered new to Caledonian Airways as G-AVKA in 1967. It was a Gatwick visitor in 1982 with TAP Air Portugal and is seen here on 2 June 1984 on a passenger charter as N106BV with Waco, Texas-based Buffalo Airways, which had bought it from TAP (hence the red/blue cheat line) in 1983. Buffalo flew cargo charters, probably including secret CIA government flights, and in the mid 1990s it operated the famous CL-44-O 'Skymonster' turboprop Guppy. N106BV flew with Buffalo until 1995, when it was sold to Azerbaijan Airlines. It eventually ended up serving various small African cargo airlines until it was scrapped at Luanda around 2007. Note the 'Buffalo Airways' fuselage titles have been painted out and replaced by the flags of the USA, Texas and a flag with a smiling sun on it that has defied all attempts to identify it! (Mike Axe)

➤ The sight of passenger-carrying Boeing 707s in the late 1980s was pretty rare at Gatwick, so the classic lines of 707-3B4C OD-AFE in August 1987 about to mix it on the ramp with the latest Airbuses and up-to-date Boeings make a great subject. Back when OD-AFE was newly delivered in 1969, Middle East Airlines (MEA) was flying a daily 707 'Cedarjet' service to Heathrow from Beirut. Apart from various leases to airlines like Nigeria Airways, Zambia Airways and Saudia, MEA's 707s were retained for services into the late 1990s thanks to hush kits that allowed operations into noise-sensitive airports like Gatwick. To show off their noise compliance, they were given a modified colour scheme with 'New Q' titles. In 1998, MEA still had eight 707s and that year OD-AFE was sold to Air Luxor as SU-BMV, sadly being written off in 2001 after a hard landing. (Author)

▲ Famous for being faster than the Boeing 707 and DC-8, the Convair 990 was just as well known for the black smoke emitted by its four GE CJ805-23B turbofans. 'Coronado' EC-CNF was a regular at Gatwick from the summer of 1975 but the 1970s' fuel crises saw Spantax withdraw its CV990s and replace them with less thirsty jets. EC-CNF was one of fourteen 149-seater Coronados flown by Spantax, making it the world's largest operator of the type in the 1970s. They flew reliably between European cities and holiday destinations in the Balearics and the Canary Islands until replaced by DC-8-63s, Boeing 737s, DC-9s and DC-10s. EC-CNF was originally delivered in 1962 to Swissair, which immediately leased it to SAS as SE-DAY. It was eventually retired in 1983 and stored at Palma alongside several others. Sister ship EC-BZO was still stored there in 2019. (Clive Grant)

◄ Once deregulation hit the airlines of the USA, Hawaiian Air began an aggressive expansion campaign and in 1983 it leased three ex-Braniff DC-8-62s for worldwide charter flights. The prize route from Honolulu to Los Angeles began in the summer of 1985 with the acquisition of five TriStars. The DC-8s were seen at Gatwick on charter services from Honolulu via Seattle, sometimes routing via Frankfurt. First visit was on the Saturday evening of 5 May 1984 when HA930 arrived in the shape of N802BN. A weekly appearance apart from a gap in June/July saw sister ship N801BN appear as well. The last recorded service was 15 September and by the following year N802BN had been returned to the lessor. Hawaiian operated a total of eight DC-8s, with some in service up until 1993. (Author)

► Pushing back from the centre finger is East German airline Interflug's magnificent Ilyushin Il-62M DDR-SEO. Interflug had first appeared at LGW in 1984, although it had the earlier Il-62 version in its fleet from 1970. They were used on routes to Moscow, Cairo, Baghdad, Dubai, Tashkent, Lagos, Luanda, Karachi, Singapore, Damascus, Havana, Hanoi and Maputo, but apparently the airline was not profitable. Luckily, the East German government thought it was important for political reasons that the state airline should be visible and therefore propped it up financially. IFL's Il-62Ms on European flights had a 168-seat all-economy, all-non-smoking layout, although seat layouts for the Il-62 showed 150 seats with a twelve-seat business class section. After German reunification, Interflug did not survive long and DDR-SEO was sold in Uzbekistan. (Author)

▲ Arriving at Gatwick in May 1982 was Boeing 727-17 G-BKCG, which was acquired by Dan-Air on a sub-lease from SAN (Servicios Aéreos Nacionales) Ecuador. It was repainted in Dan-Air colours at Lasham and eventually flew its last service for Dan-Air on 5 November 1984. After yet another repaint at Lasham, it returned to Ecuador in full TAME (Transportes Aereos Mercantiles Ecuatorianos) colours a few weeks later. Note its SAN name 'Ciudad de Guayaquil' and the crudely hand-painted registration, as well as another Dan-Air leased 727 G-BIUR in the background. (Author)

▲ Gatwick's first sighting of an all-orange Boeing 747 was on 28 February 1978 when Braniff made a pre-inaugural flight from Dallas-Ft Worth Regional Airport with civic leaders and members of the press. 'Big Orange' Boeing 747-127 N601BN arrived as BN6002; it had previously operated daily between Dallas and Honolulu since January 1971. The first appearance of Braniff's Boeing 747SP 'Special Performance' aircraft seen here at LGW was when N604BN arrived on 25 June 1980. All three 'Little Orange' Braniff 747SPs appeared at Gatwick on the non-stop service from Dallas that year. By 1981, all Braniff Boeing 747 services to Asia and Europe with the exception of the Gatwick schedule were discontinued, although they did continue serving Bogota, Buenos Aires, Santdiago and Dallas–Honolulu. Braniff packed up in 1982 but the name reappeared twice with further airline iterations. (Mike Axe)

➤ At Schiphol Airport on 26 March 1966, KLM welcomed the brand-new DC-9 PH-DNA 'Amsterdam' with much fanfare and a blast from the KLM brass band. All the other KLM DC-9s were also named after European cities except their last, which became 'Santa Monica' after the city where it was built. These early DC-9s had sixty-five seats in tourist class and eight in first class, and by 1969 the type had replaced all their Viscounts and Electras used on European routes. This is PH-DNC (first seen at Gatwick in 1966!) in 1986 when KLM was flying three daily schedules to/from Amsterdam. When the DC-9s were replaced by the Fokker 100 in 1989, the twenty-five-strong fleet had flown 770,000 hours and carried 40 million passengers. KLM had appeared at Gatwick right back to 1958 but these were nearly always Heathrow diversions with types such as Constellations, DC-7s, DC-6s, DC-3s, Convairs, Viscounts and Electras. In October 2019, KLM became the first airline to celebrate 100 years of flying under its original name. (Author)

◄ This Boeing 727-17 first flew in 1970 and in May 1982 it was sub-leased by Dan-Air from SAN Ecuador as G-BKCG and given a full repaint in Dan-Air colours at Lasham. It flew its last service for Dan-Air on 5 November 1984 and was returned to the lessor the following month. Here it is at Gatwick after it was sold to TAME Ecuador in April 1985, having been repainted in TAME (Transportes Aereos Mercantiles Ecuatorianos) colours back at Lasham. Its new registration, HC-BLV, was carried underneath the stuck-on G-BKCG. The engineless airframe was noted stored at Latacunga in 2015 and may have survived to this day. (Bob Wall)

◄ The first of Trans World Airlines' (TWA) thirty-three Lockheed TriStars arrived in 1972 and initially they flew only domestic routes. Interestingly, TWA did not use the TriStar name in its advertising, preferring to use L-1011 (spoken as El Ten Eleven). TWA's first L-1011 schedule to LGW was from Pittsburgh on 21 May 1981, and the following year an example registered N81027 commenced a five-a-week service from JFK on 25 April. TWA commenced Baltimore–Gatwick L-1011 flights in the summer of 1987. They also appeared from Philadelphia but both these routes were sold off to US Air in 1992. This is N41020 in July 1988, flying IAD–BWI–LGW–FRA–LGW–BWI–IAD. The acquisition of four leased Boeing 767-300ERs allowed TWA to remove all its L-1011s from transatlantic service from 1 June 1994. The last TWA L-1011 flight was on 3 September 1997 and the last ever TWA flight out of Gatwick was TW721 to St Louis on 1 December 2001 with Boeing 767-300ER N691LF. (Author)

➤ In 1984, the largest travel agency in Wales, Red Dragon Travel, formed Airways International Cymru with its base at Cardiff airport. The fleet initially consisted of this BAC 1-11-304AX, G-YMRU, which was flown in the modified colours of its previous operator, Quebecair, and 1-11-432FD G-AXMU, which was leased from British Island Airways until replaced by G-WLAD in late 1984. The winter 1984/85 tour season saw both 1-11s flying to Austria and Switzerland, and by 1985 the airline started to appear at Gatwick and other British airports on holiday charters. Fleet expansion followed with the addition of a Boeing 737-200 and later three 737-300s. A plan to merge with Bristol-based Paramount after Airways Cymru struggled to pay leasing fees came to nothing and the airline collapsed in January 1988. (Author)

▼ This 1960-vintage SE210 Caravelle III I-GISA was photographed at Gatwick on 21 August 1982. Altair (Linee Aeree S.p.A.) was an Italian charter airline initially based at Rome-Ciampino that commenced operations with this single Caravelle in March 1981. It moved base to Bologna and despite the economics of using a fuel-thirsty vintage jet, it bought a second Caravelle the following year. The plan was to bring European tourists to the art cities of Northern Europe but they ended up taking Italians on IT charters to Mediterranean resorts, particularly Palma, as well as UK tourists to Italy with Pegasus Travel. Three Super Caravelles were bought from Finnair in 1984 and the airline became a regular summer visitor to Gatwick, and the last ever Italian operator of the Caravelle. The purchase of either Boeing 737-200s or DC-9-50s was proposed but the company finances were in a bad way with a debt of 7 billion lire and the staff were unpaid and fed up with poor management. The airline was declared bankrupt in 1986. (Author)

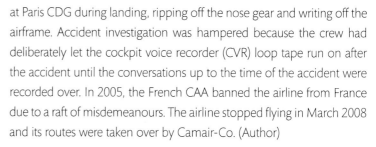

▲ First recorded at Gatwick in May 1985, Cameroon Airlines' Boeing 747-2H7B Combi TJ-CAB 'Mont Cameroun' had been delivered brand new in February 1981. Its visit was a restart of the weekly scheduled service from Douala last flown by its 707 TJ-CAA, which started in late 1981. It stopped appearing at Gatwick in the late 1990s due to horrendously low loads, sometimes just ten passengers boarded! It continued to serve Paris and Rome until 5 November 2000, when it veered off the runway at Paris CDG during landing, ripping off the nose gear and writing off the airframe. Accident investigation was hampered because the crew had deliberately let the cockpit voice recorder (CVR) loop tape run on after the accident until the conversations up to the time of the accident were recorded over. In 2005, the French CAA banned the airline from France due to a raft of misdemeanours. The airline stopped flying in March 2008 and its routes were taken over by Camair-Co. (Author)

◄ Horizon Travel, a Birmingham-based tour company, formed its own airline, Orion Airways, in late 1978 and commenced flying with four Boeing 737-200s in 1980. These first appeared at Gatwick in the spring of 1981 on IT services to the usual European resorts. In 1984, with eleven 737-200s in the fleet, Orion became the first non-US airline to order new Boeing 737-300s. In September 1986, Orion launched scheduled services from East Midlands and Birmingham to Spanish resorts and, as the enterprise grew, it leased a couple of 375-seater Airbus A300B4s from Lufthansa. The Horizon Group, which included Orion, was now ripe for picking and it was bought first by the Bass brewing enterprise, then later by the expanding Thomson Travel Group, which amalgamated it into its own Britannia Airways. (Author)

> Italian charter airline Unifly began operations in 1980 with business charters as well as overnight parcel delivery service using small aircraft. It acquired Fokker F28s I-TIDB and I-TIDI in 1984 to expand into the passenger charter business and made a deal with Alitalia whereby Unifly flew some routes for them and took over sole responsibility for others. This very early F28-1000, I-TIDB, was bought from LTU Germany and is seen here at Gatwick in July 1986 awaiting twenty-seven passengers for a charter to Pescara. In 1989 the name was changed to Unifly Express and with it came the first McDonnell Douglas MD-83. Unifly bought out Alinord and its F28s in 1990 but financial problems soon caused the airline's demise. (Jacques Guillem collection)

◀ After East African Airways broke up in 1977, the new airline of Tanzania was launched as Air Tanzania Corporation. Services commenced in June 1977 with a leased DC-9 and Air Tanzania obtained its first four-engined Boeing in the shape of this 720-022, N62215, in December 1979. It was supposed to make its first of a twice-weekly service from Dar es Salaam via Rome to Gatwick on 4 January 1980 but actually arrived in an unserviceable state on the 7th. Parts were taken to Dan-Air Engineering at Lasham for repairs while it stayed tucked away in the West Park. It eventually left for Larnaca on 8 February. It was apparent that the 720 was the wrong type for the service anyway as it could only carry twenty-nine passengers on the leg from Kilimanjaro to Gatwick! It was soon replaced by a pair of leased 707s, with the giraffe-emblazoned N762TW transiting LGW on delivery from Miami on 15 May before services restarted in June. (Author)

▲ The October 1979 Air Lanka timetable shows it was flying a twice-weekly schedule from Colombo to Gatwick via Bahrain and Frankfurt using Boeing 707s. By the early 1980s the 707s were retired, with TriStars starting to appear at Gatwick from June 1981. In total Air Lanka operated sixteen different TriStars in four types: -1, -100, -200 and -500. This is -500 4R-ULA, which flew for the airline from 1982 to 1985 before going to British Airways. Sister ship 4R-ULD was destroyed after a bomb planted by Tamil Tigers on the ground at Colombo killed twenty-one people when it arrived from Gatwick in May 1986. From 1984 to 1987, Air Lanka was flying to London with a pair of Boeing 747s as, despite the violence in Sri Lanka involving the Tamil Tigers, the island was still a popular resort for British holidaymakers. However, the airline's two letter code of 'UL' was taken to mean 'Usually Late' by those in the business! (Author)

◄ Miami-based Air Florida was founded in 1971 and first flew a pair of Boeing 707s on intra-state, low-cost services. These were replaced by Lockheed Electras and, as the airline grew, it acquired a variety of types including Boeing 727s and 737s, DC-8-62s, DC-9s and DC-10s. The airline operated a successful code share with several local airlines that all flew in Air Florida Commuter colours. The variety of types used included Convairliners, Nord 262s, CASA 212s, DH Herons, Bandeirantes and Martin 404s. Air Florida started to appear at Gatwick on a daily Miami service in 1981, using DC-10s including this one, N102TV, in full colours. Also, because the flying season in Florida was opposite to the one in Europe, Air Florida brokered deals with some European airlines to swap excess aircraft to and fro. In 1981, you could fly on your Air Europe IT holiday from Gatwick in a US-registered Boeing 737 in full Air Florida colours. (Author)

➤ British Caledonian's first Boeing 747 was wet-leased from Aer Lingus in October 1978 after its last two DC-10s on order were delayed by industrial action at the Douglas factory in Long Beach. G-BDPZ was painted in partial BCal colours and was returned to Ireland in February 1979. It wasn't until 1982 that BCal acquired another 747, this time leased from GATX for services to Lagos that commenced in May. Next to arrive was G-HUGE, seen in September 1985. This was leased from Alia Royal Jordanian for three years from March 1985 and arrived in full Alia colours (see elsewhere). BCal flew a total of five different 747-200s. In 1988 G-HUGE became part of the British Airways fleet at Gatwick after the airlines merged. (Author)

◄ The days of wide-bodied passenger-carrying three-holers have long gone at Gatwick, and indeed all over the world. In March 2020, the only Lockheed L-1011 TriStar in flying condition was N140SC, operated by Northrop Grumman Innovation Systems (formerly Orbital ATK) as the 'Stargazer' air-launch mothership. Back in the 1980s, Gatwick was full of TriStars, with examples from the USA, Canada, the British West Indies, Sri Lanka and Hong Kong as well as UK-based examples such as this British Airways TriStar Series 50 G-BEAK that had originally been delivered in 1976 as a TriStar 1. British Airtours borrowed it from BA for much of 1987 before it returned for a few more years of mainline service until it was retired in 1991. (Author)

➤ Now here is a scene that has disappeared these days. Laker's McDonnell Douglas DC-10-30 G-BGXF taxies out to the western holding point complete with a spare General Electric CF-6 engine tucked away inside its special container. Using this 'pod' was one way of getting a working engine to an aircraft stranded away from base, rather than shipping it by sea (too slow) or hiring a transport aircraft (too expensive). The broken engine was normally returned by sea. Other types to use this method included the Boeing 707, 747, DC-8, VC10 and TriStar. The method is not used any more thanks to better engine reliability and the availability of large freighters such as the Ilyushin Il-76. (Richard Vandervord)

▲ Ooops! This embarrassing incident happened in September 1988 when Northwest's (NW) Boeing 747-151 N603US was receiving some maintenance in the cargo area by the based NW engineers. They had changed a left body gear retract actuator, and while they were bleeding the system, a nose gear door dislodged the locking pin designed to prevent the gear from retracting during these cycles and the aircraft slowly collapsed on to its nose. Nothing was seriously damaged other than the feelings of the engineers aboard!

Days later, the aircraft was lifted up with a massive crane and four huge strops assisted by some airbags, allowing the nose gear to be lowered and locked. It was repaired by a Boeing Aircraft on Ground (AOG) team with help from the local NW engineers. It departed on the NWA45 schedule to MSP/LAX on the 28th. N603US continued in service with NW until June 1994 and ended up as a source of spare parts at Maxton-Laurinburg in North Carolina, where it was still visible on Google Earth in 2017. (Author)

▲ Pan American Airways' (PAA) fleet of A310s made regular appearances at Gatwick in the summer of 1991 but here is one that snuck in on 15 March 1985, probably on a demonstration flight. Carrying dual French/US markings of F-WZEC/N810PA and the name 'Clipper Berlin', it arrived from the Airbus facility at Hamburg that afternoon and was parked on Stand Cargo 1; an hour later it was off to Toulouse. Ten days later, this 214-seater was delivered to PAA in the USA. When PAA ordered twelve Airbus A310s and sixteen A320s (with options for thirty-four more) in September 1984, it was a massive blow to Boeing, which counted on PAA as a major customer. However, 'the World's most experienced airline' was heavily in debt, the A320 order was scrapped and all fifty of them were snapped up by Braniff. PAA did, however, operate twenty-one A310s between 1985 and 1991, when it filed for bankruptcy. (Mike Axe)

➤ Wholly owned by the government of Zimbabwe, Air Zimbabwe commenced scheduled flights to Gatwick from Harare with Boeing 707s on 2 April 1980. It leased a Boeing 707 from South African Airways until May 1981, when three 707-320Bs (including Z-WKS seen here) were bought from Lufthansa. In 1983, Air Zimbabwe took over the freight airline Affretair, a regular at Gatwick. Air Zimbabwe has suffered terribly with poor management and nepotism, much like the rest of Zimbabwe. In May 2017 it was added to the list of air carriers banned in the EU for failure to meet EU safety standards. In June 2018 it was reported that the airline had debts of more than $300 million and it was banned from most destinations due to threats by debtors to impound its aircraft. It was put under administration on 6 October 2018. The airline had only a single Boeing 767 operational in October 2019 but this was impounded in Johannesburg for non-payment of fees. (Author)

▼ Photographed here in June 1982 during the time Rhodesian-registered aircraft were still transitioning to the new Zimbabwe registration prefix 'Z', VP-WMJ was the only Affretair aircraft to receive a Rhodesian VP-W** registration. Affretair first operated this DC-8-55F freighter in 1972 on the Gabonese register as TR-LQR as part of a sanctions-busting operation whereby high-quality Rhodesian beef was flown to Gabon and then exported to the Middle East and Europe. From 1977 this continuing operation moved under the auspices of Cargoman, who registered the freighter in the Oman as A40-PA. With the end of the apartheid regime, the aircraft was able to operate with the Rhodesian registration Z-WMJ and was given the name 'Capt. Jack Malloch' after a famous South African-born RAF Second World War pilot who flew sanction-busting flights from Rhodesia as well as some other dubious aerial enterprises. He was killed flying his rebuilt Spitfire in March 1982. A second DC-8-55F also flew for Affretair on the Gabon register as TR-LVK, later becoming Z-WSB. Affretair became an Air Zimbabwe subsidiary in 1983 and both aircraft were regulars at Gatwick. Affretair's DC-8-55Fs were later barred from European operation by regulators, so the airline leased a turbofan-engined DC-8-71F. (Mike Axe)

▼ Working as an Air Traffic Controller with National Air Traffic Services (NATS) occasionally gave us aviation enthusiasts the opportunity to do something very special. British Airways was positioning Concorde G-BOAC from Heathrow to Gatwick on 26 July 1988 for a Bay of Biscay charter, and as the aircraft was empty, it contacted various airport/airline companies to offer free seats for this short trip. The author was very lucky to come out in the draw and set off to Heathrow for the memorable day. The lightweight take-off was very memorable but sadly we didn't get a supersonic trip round the Bay of Biscay; however, an ATCO friend was doing the radar vectoring at Gatwick and he ensured we had a nice long downwind leg, allowing us to log twenty minutes' flying time. This is Captain Mills and his cockpit crew being interviewed by the press at Gatwick. (Author)

➤ The Spanish charter airline Hispania was formed in 1982 by former employees of the failed Transeuropa. It started operations with four Caravelle 10Rs in April 1983, mainly from Germany and the UK to the usual Spanish hot spots. In 1987 Hispania added five Boeing 737-300s to the fleet and further additions included a Boeing 757 and a DC-8 leased from Nationair Canada. Gatwick-based Air Europe tried to buy out Hispania in 1989 but failed. The airline wanted to continue expansion into scheduled services but was blocked by the Spanish authorities, which wanted to protect Iberia. Despite being a reliable and safe airline highly regarded by IT companies, Hispania suffered from financial problems in the late 1980s and shut down in July 1989. (Author)

◄ Pushing back from the cargo area in April 1988 is Douglas DC-8 Series 55(F) N902R. Originally a passenger Series 55 with the SAS fleet as LN-MOH, it was converted to a freighter in 1981 and bought by Connie Kalitta Services Inc. from Volcanair in February 1988. The Kalitta airline had a convoluted family tree starting with Conrad 'Connie' Kalitta forming American International Airlines in the late 1960s. Based in Ypsilanti in Michigan, Kalitta Air is now a highly respected major freight airline that operates worldwide scheduled and other services with a fleet of Boeing 747s, 767s and 777s. It uses the R/T call sign 'Connie' and is still owned and run by Connie, who was also famous as a drag racer known as 'the Bounty Hunter'. (Author)

▼ Yet another transatlantic charter airline with 707s was Skystar International. Operating out of JFK, Skystar flew a fleet of six Boeing 707s with this one, N728Q, appearing in late September 1985. In 1986 Skystar was flying religious charters for the 'Blue Army' from JFK to Rome via Paris once a week, with a round-trip fare starting at $398. One of its 707s had a small Madonna shrine outside the cockpit door but after a trip to Las Vegas she was found to be holding playing cards with a running flush! N728Q was a 'Quiet 707' named the 'Queen of Peace' and carried additional titles 'Vive La Difference' on one of the much-modified engine nacelles. Q-707s had extended and noise-deadened nacelles built by Rohr Industries under a programme that was initiated by Shannon Engineering in Seattle but sponsored by Comtran of Texas. These Q-707s also landed with 25 degrees of flap instead of 50 degrees, so they made less noise on approach. (Author)

◄ When Virgin's first Boeing 747 appeared in June 1984, it was in this rather straightforward colour scheme but with some humour supplied by the tailfin image of a painter nearly falling off his cradle and his pot of red paint splashing down on to the fuselage. Branson liked the idea of giving the aircraft a suitable name so it was called 'Maiden Voyager', and ever since then, Virgin's aircraft have been given names, mostly connected to women. Even the registration letters, which are always G-V***, are somehow connected with the name, although some links are pretty obscure! Boeing 747-200 G-VIRG flew its first service from Gatwick to Newark on 22 June 1984 and survived in service until 2001, when it was sold in Nigeria. (Author)

◀ Photographed on 20 October 1984 taxying on to its stand in the cargo area, Boeing 707-351C 8P-CAD had small 'Caricargo' titles on the nose; this was also its radio call sign prefix. It had arrived from Port of Spain with an empty hold and departed the next day to Bridgetown with 6,279kg of freight. The airline, Caribbean Air Cargo Company Limited, which was owned by the governments of Trinidad and Tobago and Barbados, operated a pair of ex-BWIA 707s (the other was 8P-CAC) on all-freight charters from its base at Bridgetown, Barbados, to Miami, New York, Houston and Jamaica. On one flight a 707 carried 150 calves from Miami to Trinidad. Initially, the company flew Curtiss C-46 Commandos on freight runs around the Caribbean. The airline stopped flying in late 1989. (Author)

➤ The summer seasons of 1982/83 saw an Olympic Airways Airbus A300 appear every Monday, flying from and to Corfu on flight OA2634/2644. During this period, Olympic was pushing hard with its charter flights but had to compete with many non-Greek charter airlines which could operate virtually to anywhere in Greece thanks to the Greek government's 'open skies' policies. Olympic had eleven new A300s delivered starting in 1979, and it also leased a couple from Airbus. Government interference, management ineptitude and rising costs into the 2000s caused all sorts of problems for this long-lived airline, and with massive debts building, Olympic stopped flying in September 2009. (Author)

◄ Continental's first DC-10s joined the fleet in 1972 and it operated a total of forty-nine until the last ones were sold around 2002. DC-10-30 N14062 was just a year old when it was seen here in August 1986 just after the airline had emerged from Chapter 11 protection after suffering enormous financial problems and bankruptcy in 1983. The Houston to London service, at that time Continental's only transatlantic route, had started in 1985. The airline's parent company (Texas Air Group) bought out People Express, New York Air and Frontier in 1987, doubling the scale of Continental's operations. It was under Chapter 11 protection again from 1990 until 1993 and the airline was eventually absorbed into United in 2012 to make the world's biggest airline. The 'COA' code disappeared after the final arrival of a 777 from Tokyo to Houston in March 2012. (Author)

➤ CTA (Compagnie de Transports Aérien) was a Swiss airline based in Geneva. It was formed in late 1978 from the ashes of SATA, which had folded after one of its Caravelles had crashed. It was able to quickly change the titles on the three remaining SATA Caravelles (its DC-8s were disregarded) and commenced European charters in November. Caravelle 10R HB-ICQ, seen in August 1986, was one of the original three from 1978 along with HB-ICN and ICO. With noise restrictions looming, after ten years flying Caravelles, CTA needed more modern jets and its first MD-87 arrived in 1988. By the summer of 1989, the Caravelles had earned a rest and had all been sold. HB-ICQ made return visits from November 1989 as TC-ASA with Istanbul Airlines. (Author)

▲ Showing signs of some serious paint stripping outside the BCal maintenance area in June 1985 is Air Zaire's Douglas DC-10-30 9Q-CLT. One of two delivered new to Air Zaire, this aircraft (named 'Mont Ngafula') only lasted a year with the airline before it was sold to Security Pacific Financing in June 1985 and immediately leased to British Caledonian. It arrived at LGW as 9Q-CLT and after repainting became G-NIUK. Air Zaire's other DC-10 9Q-CLI was also a Gatwick visitor back in 1973. Famous (infamous?) for its huge delays and poor management, Air Zaire had to sell 9Q-CLT to pay off debts. The airline was pretty much run for the benefit of President Mobuto and his cronies, who liked to commandeer the DC-10s and 747 for shopping trips to Paris and Brussels. In the early 1990s, Air Zaire ordered two MD-11s and two MD-80s, but with debts running into millions, the orders were cancelled and the airline finally expired in 1995. (Author)

◄ Photographed from the Ground Movement Control position in the control tower in the summer of 1985 is Air Atlantis' Boeing 707-382B CS-TBA. Air Atlantis was set up as a charter arm of the Portuguese national airline TAP Air Portugal in 1985, with TAP being the sole shareholder. Both Boeing 707s and 727s were leased from the parent company and commenced IT operations in June 1985. By the summer of 1988, Air Atlantis had its own fleet of new Boeing 737-300s and the older 737-200s that had replaced the fuel-thirsty 707s and 727s were gradually sold off. Note the ancient DH Comet G-APMB 'Wingless Wonder' that was used to train tug drivers as well as ground staff, who positioned vehicles such as passenger steps and catering trucks. (Author)

▲ Air New Zealand (ANZ) received the first of five Boeing 747-219Bs as DC-10 replacements in 1981 and named them after historic Maori canoes. ZK-NZV, seen here, was its first 747 and was named 'Aotea'. This stunning and historic shot shows ZK-NZV arriving at Gatwick on 26 August 1982 having flown the first of a twice-weekly service to Gatwick from Auckland via Tahiti and Los Angeles. Note the special additional 'London – All the way with The Pacific Number One' markings alongside the image of a soldier from the Household Cavalry. On 1 April 1984, ANZ made the first non-stop 747 flight from Auckland to Los Angeles as part of a weekly one-stop service to London. The journey time of twenty-four hours was the fastest from New Zealand to the UK. From April 1991, the route was upgraded with the 747-400 and the author made a return trip to LAX in ZK-NBU early in 1994 for the princely sum of £134 return (staff standby rate). However, on 24 November 1994, the airline transferred its London flights to Heathrow. (Glen Reid collection)

◄ There are now no scheduled passenger services by DC-10s; the last to operate one was Biman Bangladesh Airlines, which made their final DC-10 service from Dhaka to Birmingham via Kuwait in February 2014. There it made some farewell flights for enthusiasts before heading home for scrapping. Back in the 1980s Gatwick was full of DC-10s with based aircraft from BA, BCal and Laker as well as examples from around the world. Garuda Indonesia flew six different DC-10s to Gatwick along with later Boeing 747s for many years. This is DC-10-30 PK-GIF 'Sulawesi' in September 1980. In 1982 the twice-weekly 747 service from Jakarta to Gatwick stopped at Singapore, Bangkok, Abu Dhabi, Zurich and Frankfurt on one service and Singapore, Bangkok, Jeddah and Paris CDG on the other. (Author)

➤ Gatwick could still see passenger Boeing 707s into the mid 1980s and Sobelair's 707-373C OO-SBU was a nice one to shoot in August 1986. Société Belge de Transports Par Air SA began operations with a single Douglas DC-3 in 1947. The following year, the Belgian national airline bought a controlling interest, and from 1960 the airline moved from scheduled services to concentrate on Mediterranean charters. By 1971 Sobelair had grown and had obtained its first jetliner in the shape of an ex-SABENA Caravelle. It acquired its first of ten 707s in 1974, some of them remaining in service until 1988. This 707 was still flying as an E-8C with the USAF in 2019. Sobelair was declared bankrupt on 19 January 2004. A Belgian business magazine said, 'Sobelair had everything it needed to succeed but because of amateurish management, this bloodless company has been consigned to the cemetery, which is already overflowing with defunct Belgian airlines.' (Author)

◀ The author was very fortunate to be on duty when this Boeing 747-2D3B Combi, JY-AFB 'Princess Haya', arrived on a nice sunny day on delivery to British Caledonian in March 1985. Still in full Alia Royal Jordanian colours, it was initially parked in the cargo area before going into the hangars and emerging as G-HUGE. BCal had needed extra capacity due to new routes to Riyadh and New York starting, so a pair of second-hand DC-10s and this 747 were sourced quickly. JY-AFB was flown to Gatwick direct from Amman on 18 March in just over five hours. G-HUGE, which had a large port-side freight door, was rolled out complete with the name 'Andrew Carnegie – The Scottish American philanthropist' and commenced schedules to New York that summer. (Author)

➤ Originally delivered to British Airtours at Gatwick in April 1981, Boeing 737-236 G-BGJL was named 'Goldfinch'. It was renamed 'River Orrin' when it was given the revised colour scheme seen here around 1985. The author photographed it taxying away from the cargo area in July 1985, just weeks before it was so tragically destroyed after an abandoned take-off at Manchester Ringway on 22 August. An uncontained fire in No. 1 engine spread to the wing and the ensuing fire caused the deaths of fifty-three passengers and two crew. The accident caused a massive rethink in coping with such incidents as well as replacement of cabin furnishings that had caused extremely toxic fumes to be released when burned. (Author)

➤ A nice trio of British Island Airways BAC 1-11s parked up on the 140 stands in May 1983. Closest to the camera is this 1969 Series 416EK, G-CBIA, which had had a busy life by the time it was bought by BIA in May 1979. Originally delivered to Autair at Luton, it spent time in Nigeria, Singapore and Indonesia before returning to the UK. In 1978, BIA had bought four second-hand 1-11s to start operating IT services from Gatwick. After a rename to Air UK in 1980, the BIA name reappeared in 1982 purely for the IT market. Note that G-CBIA is fitted with hush kits on its Spey engines. The whole BIA 1-11 fleet were hush-kitted over a period of a year using Rolls-Royce kits fitted by Dan-Air Engineering. (Author)

◄ Most readers will remember what a BCal BAC 1-11 looked like in full colours, so here is one in the airline's fleet that looked somewhat different. The colour scheme belongs to the short-lived charter airline Air Manchester that flew BAC 1-11 G-SURE for around three months. One-Eleven Series 416EK G-AVOF, seen here in December 1983 in the BCal maintenance area at Gatwick, was supposed to be Air Manchester's second 1-11 (as G-BMAN) but was never delivered as the airline had folded, so it was used by BCal in this livery from November 1983 until January 1984. The curved line on the fuselage just forward of the nose wheel door can be seen on many airliners. It shows the tug driver the maximum limit of the angle of the tow bar at which he can manoeuvre the aircraft without damaging the nose leg. (Author)

▼ At one time in the 1990s, American Trans Air was the largest charter airline in the USA. Founded in 1973 in Indianapolis, Indiana, it started out flying three Boeing 720s for the Ambassadair Travel Club and expanded into airline charters in 1981. A total of eight Boeing 707s were bought initially and these were traded in to Boeing in part exchange for Boeing 727s and TriStars. American Trans Air also acquired DC-10s but a shortage of available aircraft forced a switch to TriStars in 1985. The airline's 707s, DC-10s and TriStars all appeared at Gatwick on transatlantic charters, including this 707-323C, N8416, which it leased then bought from American Airlines in 1983. Here it is turning on to a stand at the Satellite Terminal in the summer of 1983. (Author)

➤ The first ever Boeing 707 to land at Gatwick was a Pan American Boeing 707 that diverted in from Heathrow in February 1959. Pan Am 707s appeared on regular affinity charters in the late 1960s and '70s but their first scheduled daily jetliner service to Gatwick did not start until 2 July 1980 with a service from Houston with TriStars. Boeing 747s also appeared on this route until it was sold to Continental in 1983. Appearances of Douglas DC-10s, such as N81NA seen here in August 1982, were pretty rare and were probably a TriStar replacement on the Houston route. This aircraft had previously visited while flying for National in November 1979. (Author)

◄ This very clean Boeing 707-351C N2215Y in full Westar International Airways colours was seen in April 1984 taxying inbound after Westar had bought it in November 1983 while still called Westar Charter. The airline, which was based in Houston, Texas, also flew 707-321C N732Q. Both 707s flew ad hoc passenger charters until they were both passed to Skystar in late 1985. N2215Y returned to Gatwick in July 1986 while operating for Skystar/Tropical Airlines (see elsewhere). Compare the engine cowlings on this pre-hush kit version to those in the picture of the Skystar/Tropical colours. Built in 1967, N2215Y was originally delivered to Northwest Orient as N375US and through its life it was flown by an impressive number of operators, including British West Indian, Skystar International, Buffalo Airways (USA) and Heavylift Cargo Airlines. (Author)

▲ Perhaps not such a popular destination these days due to security fears, Israel was a regular destination in the 1980s with Arkia as well as Sun d'Or and MAOF flying holiday charters to the UK. Boeing 727-95 4X-BAE was sub-leased by Arkia from Avianca Colombia for a year in 1984/85, hence the non-standard red colours. It was the only 727 flown by Arkia. It was delivered via Miami and Gatwick to Tel Aviv early in May 1984 before it reappeared on services, although Arkia normally used Boeing 737-200s and 707s on flights to Gatwick in the 1980s. This aircraft was no stranger to Gatwick, having appeared with Dan-Air as G-BFGM in the late 1970s and later as EI-BUI with Club Air in 1987. Arkia brought Boeing 757s to Gatwick in 2000/01 for summer charters, and in November 2018 Arkia was the first airline to receive the long-range Airbus 321LR, which can fly 4,000 miles non-stop. (Author)

◄ Tucked round the far end of the cul-de-sac of the Satellite Terminal was a super spot for a picture, especially if you climbed up the steps to the jetway for a better angle. Here is Boeing 707-331B N8733 of Worldwide Airlines on 19 August 1984; it was on a lease from the Aviation Sales Co. to well-established Chicago-based tour operator Carefree Vacations, which had set up a subsidiary company called Worldwide Airlines Inc. to operate its charters from Chicago to Hawaii, Mexico and the Caribbean. It leased three Stage 1 noise compliant 707s between April and June 1984 with N8733 entering service with Worldwide on 2 June 1984. With noise restrictions looming, on 31 December 1984, one day before the Federal Aviation Administration (FAA) deadline, Carefree entered into a contract to purchase a hush kit for one of its 707s with options for two more kits. However, it was unable to pay for the kits, so the 707s were sold. (Author)

➤ This is Douglas DC-8-62 SE-DDU 'Maro' taxying outbound on 22 July 1982 for flight OE311 to Boston after a transit/refuelling stop for the 186 passengers who had arrived from Athens via Rome Ciampino. The aircraft was bought new by Scandinavian Airlines (SAS) in August 1967 and was leased by Arista International Airlines (AIA) in June 1982 but was returned to SAS the following January. Founded in July 1981, Arista was based at JFK airport in New York and commenced operations in April 1982, including transatlantic charters to Athens, Vienna and Tel Aviv, using a small fleet of leased DC-8s. It used five in total but only ever had a maximum of three at any one time. The airline ceased flying in the summer of 1984. (Author)

▼ The Arrow Air fleet of 707s, DC-8s and DC-10s became a regular sight at Gatwick during the mid 1980s. This is DC-10 N902JW in July 1984 after push back round the back of the Satellite Terminal. Note that the paintwork is looking tired and also note something that you never see these days … brown nicotine stains along the lower fuselage behind an air vent. It is easy to forget that smoking was the norm aboard airliners for most of the twentieth century. Oh, the joy of travel when you were allocated a space alongside heavy smokers down the back of a wide-body jet for a seven-hour transatlantic flight! After complaints by, among others, the flight attendants' unions, the first airline to ban smoking on domestic flights was Qantas in 1987. The USA followed in 1988, banning smoking on flights of two hours or less. In 2000, smoking on all US-registered airliners was banned and over the years all airlines have adopted this policy, although China only followed as late as October 2017. (Author)

◄ Always smartly turned out were the Tupolev Tu-134s of Yugoslav charter airline Aviogenex. Formed as the air transport division 'Genex' of Generalexport, the airline was renamed Aviogenex and flew its first Tu-134 service in April 1969 from its base at Belgrade to Düsseldorf. Aviogenex first visited Gatwick in October that year, and during the 1980s, Aviogenex was the busiest charter airline in Yugoslavia and operated twelve Tu-134s in total, all of which visited LGW. This is Tu-134 YU-AJD in October 1988. From 1983 the airline also flew Boeing 727-200s and 737s to Gatwick but as Yugoslavia disintegrated in the 1990s, so did its international tourism and consequently the airline. It was forced to either sell or retire all of its aircraft except a single Boeing B737-200. (Author)

➤ Awaiting line-up clearance at holding point Alpha North on 4 February 1983 is CP Air's colourful McDonnell Douglas DC-10 Series 30 C-GCPC en route to Toronto. Named 'Empress of Amsterdam' on the nose, C-GCPC had been built in 1978 and, other than a lease to VARIG in Brazil, it stayed with CP Air until it was transferred to Canadian Airlines International in April 1987. Originally Canadian Pacific Air Lines, the CP Air title and colours were adopted on its fleet in 1968; even its sole-surviving Douglas DC-3 Dakota, which was used for pilot training, received the new colours. The 1970s saw the fleet expand with DC-10s and Boeing 747s, both types appearing regularly on summer charters at Gatwick. In December 1986, Pacific Western Airlines bought CP Air for $CAN 300 million and merged the two airlines into Canadian Airlines International. (Author)

▲ Wearing its 'fixed' registration 9G-ANA, Ghana Airways' colourful McDonnell Douglas DC-10 was delivered to Accra in February 1983 for use on the airline's long-range services to London Heathrow (via Rome) and to Amsterdam, Frankfurt, Douala, Jeddah, Niamey and Libreville. It replaced Ghana Airways' Vickers VC10, which had been retired in 1980; another VC10 was destroyed in an Israeli raid on Beirut. 9G-ANA made its first visit to Gatwick on 30 March 1984 on a diversion from Heathrow. From June 1984, insufficient traffic combined with a huge debt forced Ghana Airways to lease this DC-10 to Caribbean Airways for two days a week for services between Gatwick and Barbados. Other aircraft leased to Caribbean were DC-10s from BCal and Martinair as well as a 747 from Cargolux. Eventually these flights were flown by Caribbean Airways' own stretched DC-8, 8P-PLC. (Author)

◄ Just creeping in to the thirty-year cut off since Gatwick opened is Paramount Airways. Based at Bristol with an initial fleet of two leased MD-83s from 1987, it specialised in IT charters to Spanish resorts but soon expanded to other Mediterranean destinations, flying on behalf of various tour operators. This expansion required additional MD-83s and the lease of a Boeing 737-33A. In October 1988, Boeing 737-2Q8 G-BKMS joined the fleet after Amber Airways was acquired. An interesting type appeared in June 1989 when Boeing 727 N289AT was leased from American Trans Air for summer services from Gatwick. As with so many potentially successful charter airlines, Paramount went into administration in August 1989 with massive money problems. (Author)

▲ After serving with TWA for thirteen years, this DC-9 Series 15 was bought by British Midland Airways (BMA) in November 1979, registered G-BMAB and given the name 'Ulster'. Seen here at LGW in October 1981, it remained in BMA service until 1994, when it was sold in Colombia. Interesting fact: BMA was the only British airline to operate DC-9s (as opposed to the MD-80 series). Air Traffic Controllers loved the 'short' DC-9s because of their impressive rate of climb; one pilot recalled that his 'pocket rocket' departed from Heathrow and crossed over the Burnham reporting point (about 7 miles out) at 16,000ft! The Heathrow ATCOs also loved them because of the leftover hot breakfasts that appeared in the control tower half an hour after landing ... (Author)

BIBLIOGRAPHY

Charles Woodley (2014). *Gatwick Airport: The First 50 Years*. The History Press.

Phil Lo Bao (1989). *An illustrated History of British European Airways*. Browcom Group Plc.

Phil Lo Bao (1992). *Airlines and Airliners: Trident*. The Aviation Data Centre.

Phil Lo Bao (undated). *Airlines and Airliners: The De Havilland Comet*. The Aviation Data Centre.

Phil Lo Bao (1993). *Airlines and Airliners: VC10*. The Aviation Data Centre.

Phil Lo Bao (undated). *Airlines and Airliners: BAC One-Eleven*. The Aviation Data Centre.

B.I. Hengi (1999). *Airlines Remembered: Over 200 Airlines of the Past, Described and Illustrated in Colour*. Midland Publishing.

B.I. Hengi (1994 and 1997). *Airlines Worldwide*. Midland Publishing.

Klaus Vomhof (2001). *Leisure Airlines of Europe*. SCOVAL Publishing.

A.C. Merton Jones (2000). *British Independent Airlines 1946–1976*. The Aviation Hobby Shop.

Roy Blewett (various dates). *Survivors*. Gatwick Aviation Society in association with Complete Classics.

Captain Arthur H. Larkman (2008). *Dan-Air, an Airline and its People*. GMS Enterprises.

David Thaxter (2009). *The History of British Caledonian Airways 1928–1988*.

David Thaxter, Peter Hillman, Stuart Jessup, Adrian Morgan, Tony Morris, Guus Ottenhof, Michael Roch (2004). *More than Half a Century of Soviet Transports*. The Aviation Hobby Shop.

Bob Shives and Bill Thompson (1984). *Airlines of North America*. Crest Line.

Graham M. Simons (1993). *The Spirit of Dan-Air*. GMS Enterprises.

Gatwick Aviation Society (1967 onwards). *Hawkeye, Gatwick Aviation Society Journal*. Gatwick Aviation Society.

Allan J. Wright (1996). *The British World Airlines Story*. Midland Publishing Ltd.

Ricky-Dene Halliday (1992). *World Airline Colours of Yesteryear*. Aviation Data Centre Ltd.

John King and Geoff Tait (1980). *Golden Gatwick: 50 Years of Aviation*. Royal Aeronautical Society.

Scott Henderson (1998). *Silent Swift Superb: The Story of the Vickers VC10*. Scoval Publishing Ltd.

Scott Henderson (2015). *The Pictorial History of BOAC and Associated Airlines*. Scoval Publishing Ltd.

Geoffrey Cuthbert (1987). *Flying to the Sun (Britannia Airways)*. Hodder and Stoughton.

Malcolm Porter (2004). *CL-44 Swingtail: The CL-44 Story*. Air-Britain Publications.

Tony Pither (1998). *The Boeing 707, 720 and C-135*. Air-Britain Publications.

David Hedges (undated). *The Eagle Years 1948–1968*. The Aviation Hobby Shop.

A. Avrane (1981). *Sud Est Caravelle*. Jane's Publishing Co.

Terry Waddington (1996). *Douglas DC-8*. World Transport Press Inc.

Timothy Walker (2000). *The First Jet Airliner: The Story of the De Havilland Comet*. Scoval Publishing.